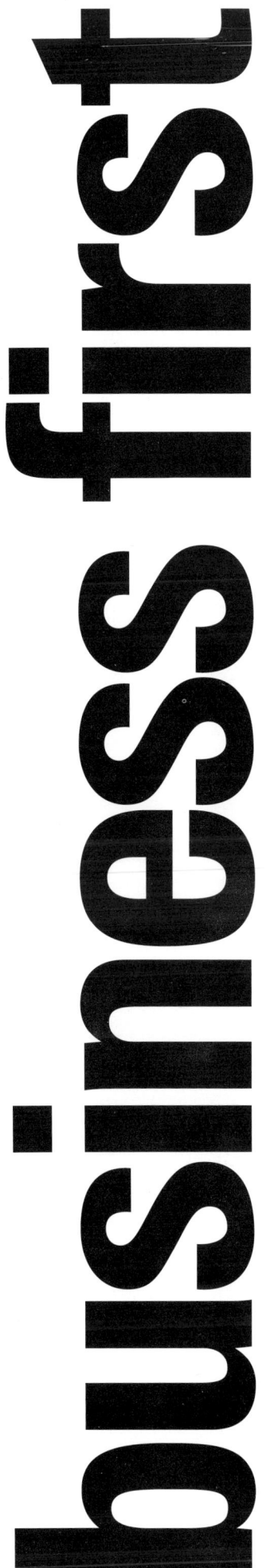

A First Course in Business English

Colin Benn
Paul Dummett

HEINEMANN

Heinemann International
A division of Heinemann Publishers (Oxford) Ltd
Halley Court, Jordan Hill, Oxford OX2 8EJ

OXFORD   LONDON   EDINBURGH
MADRID   ATHENS   BOLOGNA   PARIS
MELBOURNE   SYDNEY   AUCKLAND   SINGAPORE   TOKYO
IBADAN   NAIROBI   HARARE   GABORONE
PORTSMOUTH (NH)

ISBN 0 435 28071 6

Illustrated by:
Richardson Studios pp. 28, 30, 42, 66, 83, 84, 85, 98, 100
Angela Lumbley pp. 12, 21, 44, 48, 50
Martin Sanders pp. 2, 7, 10, 13, 14, 22, 35, 36, 37, 49, 51

Acknowledgements
The authors would like to thank Tony Conway and the staff of Godmer House School of English for their help with this book.

Designed by Richard Boxall Design Associates

Printed and bound in Great Britain by
Thomson Litho Ltd, East Kilbride, Scotland

92 93 94 95 96 97 10 9 8 7 6 5 4 3 2 1

CONTENTS

Page

Contents Chart iv

Student's Notes vi

Teacher's Notes vii

Unit 1   A Personal Presentation...................................... 1
Unit 2   A Job Description 3
Unit 3   A Business Trip 8
Unit 4   Fact Finding 13
Unit 5   An Invoice from a Supplier.................................... 15
Unit 6   A Situation Report 22
Unit 7   Entertaining a Client 27
Unit 8   An Important Message 30
Unit 9   A Look at the Figures 36
Unit 10   Saying the Right Thing 41
Unit 11   A Manufacturing Process 44
Unit 12   A New Product 49
Unit 13   A Five-Year Plan 53
Unit 14   Making an Arrangement 57
Unit 15   A Progress Report 59
Unit 16   A Personnel Problem... 64
Unit 17   A Joint Venture 68
Unit 18   Taking Part in a Meeting...................................... 72
Unit 19   Correspondence 74
Unit 20   Review.. 77

Pronunciation Practice 79

Diagnostic Grammar Test 80

Grammar Reference and Practice 81

Tapescripts and Key 107

Irregular Verbs 126

Pronunciation Chart 127

Word List 128

CONTENTS CHART

	UNIT	TASKS/FUNCTIONS
1.	A Personal Presentation	Presenting yourself
2.	A Visit to a Company	Describing jobs/responsibilities Expressing likes and dislikes
3.	A Business Trip (Sports Equipment)	Spelling Requesting Asking for/checking information
4.	Fact Finding	Question practice
5.	An Invoice from a Supplier (Industrial Supplies)	Numbers Expressing quantity Checking facts Reacting
6.	A Situation Report (Tourism)	Describing trends Writing memos
7.	Entertaining a Client	Restaurant language
8.	An Important Message (Cosmetics/Property)	Telephoning Getting through Leaving messages
9.	A Look at the Figures (Pharmaceuticals)	Describing graphs Giving reasons
10.	Saying the Right Thing	Everyday expressions
11.	A Manufacturing Process (Match Production)	Describing processes and methods Giving instructions
12.	A New Product (Packaging)	Describing products and their features Giving a presentation
13.	A Five-Year Plan (Car Manufacturing)	Talking about plans Predicting
14.	Making an Arrangement	Arranging meetings
15.	A Progress Report	Talking about company history Describing recent developments
16.	A Personnel Problem	Giving opinions Agreeing and disagreeing Problem solving
17.	A Joint Venture (Audio Equipment)	Negotiating
18.	Taking Part in a Meeting	Presenting an argument and running a meeting
19.	Correspondence	Writing letters
20.	Review	Survival English and vocabulary review

GRAMMAR	READING	VOCABULARY
Present Simple	Profile of a company chairman	Countries and nationalities
Present Simple, **like + -ing** **must, have/need to**	Job advertisements	Company organization
can, could, would like	A letter requesting information	People and buildings
Past Simple	Technical data	Dates and times
Present Continuous Comparison of Adjectives	A memo	Adjectives and nouns
will **ask/tell**	Telecommunications	Money
Past Simple **because** **because of/due to**	A campaign plan	Sales and marketing
Present Passive Imperatives	A production system	Sizes, shapes and materials
Superlatives	An advertising brief	Verbs and nouns
Infinitive of Purpose **going to/will** 1st Conditional	A profit and loss account	Finance
Past Passive Present Perfect **some, all, none, many, few,** etc.	An internal report	Personal characteristics
should	A training plan	Idioms
1st and 2nd Conditionals	An agency agreement	Phrasal verbs

STUDENT'S NOTES

HOW TO USE THIS BOOK

This book is a complete course for students at a low level who want to use English in their work.

Units 1 to 20 have:

- Vocabulary and useful expressions
- Listening practice
- Speaking practice
- Reading practice
- Writing practice

At the back of the book you can find:

- A grammar test
- Grammar explanations and exercises
- Pronunciation practice
- A word list (with space to write the meanings)
- Answers to all the exercises
- Tapescripts of the listening passages

The only other book you will need is a dictionary. We recommend both English-English and English-your language dictionaries.

SELF-STUDY

If you use the book without a teacher:

1. Use the language boxes to help with the speaking activities and record yourself if possible.
2. Check what you said by looking at the *Common Errors* boxes and at the *Grammar Reference and Practice* section.
3. With listening exercises, play the tape two or more times and check your understanding with the *Tapescripts and Key*.
4. Use the *Reading and Vocabulary* sections to learn important business words and expressions.

TEACHER'S NOTES

UNITS 1-20

Business First contains 20 units, each being approximately one hour's teaching material. Of these 20 units, five (1, 4, 7, 10, and 14) deal with everyday rather than specifically business language.

READING AND VOCABULARY

Thirteen of the units are followed by a *Reading and Vocabulary* section. These are designed either to stand alone or to follow on from the units. They can be used as homework exercises or in class.

A TYPICAL UNIT

A typical unit contains:

- Listening practice
- Vocabulary work
- Language boxes
- Grammar pointers
- Controlled practice exercises
- Varied activities and tasks
- Opportunities for pair and group work
- Common Errors summaries

LISTENING PRACTICE

The listening exercises include English spoken by a variety of native and non-native speakers. Where a listening activity has two parts, we recommend playing the tape two or more times.

VOCABULARY WORK

There are exercises in many units which deal specifically with a new area of vocabulary. New words may also occur in the listening and reading material within a unit. Depending on the time available and the level/needs of your students, you may wish to pre-teach some of these words. But remember that students also need to develop strategies for coping with unfamiliar words, for example, prediction, guessing from context, getting round the problem word, etc., strategies which are vital when faced with authentic material.

LANGUAGE BOXES

These provide the student with a summary of useful phrases and formulae appropriate to the task, for example 'Describing Trends'.

GRAMMAR

A full *Grammar Reference* section covering all the points that arise in the units is to be found at the back of the book. It contains explanations, examples and practice activities. It can help either to prepare students for a new unit or to consolidate after it. In this way the material is suited to a range of levels from the very elementary student upwards. Throughout the units, grammar pointers refer students to the relevant part of the grammar section, encouraging them to do their own research.

CONTROLLED PRACTICE

Although grammar explanations have not been included in the main units (see above), controlled practice of grammatical structures has. Rather than being purely mechanical, these exercises provide practice which is realistic and motivating, and which recycles vocabulary learned in previous units.

TASKS

Each unit leads towards the performance of a task or information exchange, for example, telephoning for a list of addresses or taking part in a meeting. As far as possible the tasks should be carried out as if they were real, without your intervention. Your role in these activities, especially in a final task, is to observe (or record on tape) and make a note of the mistakes students make, or problems they have, for correction and feedback afterwards. One useful technique is reformulation, i.e. asking the students to do a second version of the activity after correction.

STUDENT A AND B

Some activities involve two students reading different information. Because both sets of information are on the same page, students should cover up the part which is not relevant to them.

COMMON ERRORS

A box at the end of each unit contains a summary of errors that students typically make with the language covered in that unit. The purpose of these boxes is to confront the students with errors which they may be making unwittingly and to encourage them to think about the way the language works.

PRONUNCIATION

To enable the students to work on their pronunciation:
1. A full word list (pages 128–133) gives phonetic symbols for each word.
2. A pronunciation chart (page 127) shows the sounds of English and their phonetic symbols.
3. A pronunciation exercise (page 79) groups words by sound. These words are also on tape so that students can listen and repeat.

LISTEN AND SPEAK

At the end of units 4, 7, 10 and 14, there are one-sided dialogues recorded on the tape with enough space for students to have a conversation with the speaker. These exercises can be done open-class, or by the student on his own, and are intended to consolidate the language learned in the preceding units.

WRITING

One unit (19) is devoted to letter writing, but there are several writing tasks in the *Reading and Vocabulary* section (including memos, reports, plans, etc.).

A NOTE ON BRITISH AND AMERICAN ENGLISH

In this book you will find a wide range of nationalities using English and, for this reason, the English used is international rather than British or American. The spellings are British, except where an American text is used (for example, A Conference Center in Unit 4). On the whole the grammar and vocabulary in the book is common to both dialects, and where there is a significant difference the American is given in brackets (for example, in Company Organization in Unit 2). The settings and topics are international, and the cassette carries a variety of clear accents.

UNIT BY UNIT

UNIT 1

Talking about yourself: Students get a second chance to do this activity with the help of the language box and any corrections you want to make. Encourage students to ask questions if they want to. While each student is talking, the other students should make notes.

UNIT 2

A visit to a company: Students can compare summaries in pairs.

A job description: Students can each find out about one or two jobs from the dictionary and tell the others so they can make notes.

Introducing someone: Students can start by asking each other about their jobs in pairs. They can then introduce each other to the rest of the group.

Job priorities: Students can compare/discuss their list of priorities with each other in pairs/groups.

Your job: Pair work.

UNIT 3

Company names: Students can spell names to each other in pairs, adding any other company names they can think of.

Asking for help: Students work in closed pairs; the exercise is then checked in open pairs.

UNIT 4

Where is it?: Students can follow up this activity by adding a few buildings of their own (e.g. their office etc.).

Fact finding: An alternative procedure (if time is short) is for Student A only to read the information about the Royal Hotel and use this for the role play.

UNIT 5

Ordering supplies: Students may need to listen two or three times and help each other by sharing their information.

Placing an order: Pair work.

UNIT 6
Investing in property: Group work.

UNIT 7
Explaining the menu: Pair work.

UNIT 8
On the phone: Follow the same procedure as for Listen and Speak in Unit 4.

UNIT 9
Describing performance: Check the exercise by questioning students e.g. "What happened to output/inflation last month?".

A look at the figures: Working in pairs, students can each explain one bar chart to their partner. Students choosing topic 3 for their own presentation can use the information on page 36.

UNIT 11
Instructions: Pair work.

A manufacturing process: The follow-up description can be done as pair work.

Brainstorming: Put students in discussion groups according to the topic they have chosen. For a class discussion, have each group summarize their thoughts/ideas for the others.

UNIT 12
Presenting a product: Some students may like to use one of the bottle designs in the previous activity for their presentation.

UNIT 13
Plans and intentions: Pair work.

A five-year plan: Students can work in pairs to answer the two questions.

UNIT 14
Arranging a meeting: The idea is for students to try making an arrangement without first seeing the language box. They should cover the rest of the page. Arrangements 3 and 4 can be done as role play.

UNIT 15

Company history: The events are already in order. All students need to do is to supply the dates and the correct verb form. They can then talk about their company's (country's) history in pairs.

Survey results: Pair work.

A progress report: This can be done in pairs with each student completing a different fact sheet and then asking for the information to complete the other one. Start by focusing the students' attention on the questions they need to ask and the verb form each question requires. If you are teaching a group, it helps to put all Student A's and all Student B's together after they have read about their project to compare their factsheets.

UNIT 16

Giving opinions: This can take the form of a group discussion, with each student choosing a different topic and asking the others for their opinions. You might like to start by going through the language box open-class as an example.

A personnel problem: Role play.

A puzzle: Students can discuss this problem first in pairs and then in groups to try and find the best solution.

UNIT 17

Mini negotiations: Pair work.

UNIT 18

Taking part in a meeting: Make sure students are well-prepared. The main part of the meeting should be taken up with discussing the criteria for their choice. You might like to ask one of the students to act as chairperson and draw up an agenda with this as the first item.

UNIT 19

Types of letter: Draw students' attention to the various conventions and useful formulae e.g. Yours faithfully, I look forward to hearing from you.

UNIT 20

This unit is for revision and practice.

1 A PERSONAL PRESENTATION

You are attending a one-week course on Personnel Management. It's the first day. Say a few words about yourself (personal details, your work, and interests). First think about what you want to say and make notes to help you.

Write down the occupations and interests of other people.

Name	Occupation	Interests
Paolo Mazzoni	systems analyst	politics, windsurfing

Now write a short description of yourself and your work. This time use the language box to help you.

Talking about yourself

I'm...	I'm a...
I am 32 years old.	I work for XBC as a...
I'm from...	XBC is a small/large company/group.
I was born in...	It is based in...
I live in/near...	We produce/design/export/supply...
I'm married/single.	I'm interested in...
I have three children.	I like...
	I play...

A PERSONAL PRESENTATION

Now give the presentation again.

Common Errors

>   *am*   *old*
> I ~~have~~ 32 years ∧.
>   *a*
> I am ∧ saleswoman.
>   *skiing*
> I like ~~ski~~.
>   *was*
> I ∧ born in Stockholm.
>   *live*
> I ~~am~~ ~~living~~ 20 minutes from Lyon.

CHECK YOUR GRAMMAR: PAGE 82.

PROFILE OF A COMPANY CHAIRMAN

AT 15 he was a shop assistant. At 20 he started his own repair company. Today at 44 he is one of the richest men in the U.K. Alan Dury is the chairman of DURANCO plc, the company which sells TV's, video recorders, personal computers and hi-fi's at prices lower than anyone else's.

Duranco is based at Solihull in Birmingham, but it manufactures most of its products in Taiwan. The main reason for the success of the company is an excellent marketing team which is always looking for, and finding, the right product at the right time. Dury doesn't have an office, but runs the company from home.

With 150 million shares in DURANCO he is a rich man, but he doesn't like to show it. He drives a family car and lives in a medium-sized house in the suburbs of Birmingham, where he was born. In fact he is not very different from the millions of people who buy his products every day.

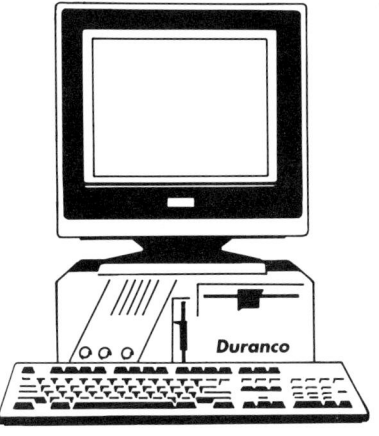

In what ways is Alan Dury an unusual company chairman?

COUNTRIES AND NATIONALITIES

He is a company chairman from Britain. He's British. (He speaks English.)

Study these.

Country	Nationality
Japan	Japanese
Portugal	Portuguese
Sweden	Swedish
Turkey	Turkish
U.S.A.	American
Russia	Russian
Brazil	Brazilian
Nigeria	Nigerian
Germany	German
Saudi Arabia	Saudi
Pakistan	Pakistani
France	French
Switzerland	Swiss
Greece	Greek
The Netherlands	Dutch

Now try these.

Country	Nationality
Australia	
Belgium	
Spain	
Kuwait	
Canada	
Mexico	
China	
Italy	
Singapore	
Denmark	

What languages do they speak in these countries? What currencies do they use?

Mark where we put the stress when we say these words.

e.g. Austrália   Austrálian

2

2   A JOB DESCRIPTION

WHO DOES WHAT?

The functions of a general manager are to: make decisions
supervise staff, and
solve problems.

Look at the list of functions below and decide who does what. Add any more you can think of.

negotiate agreements   visit clients
arrange appointments   type letters
deal with inquiries   attend meetings
present new products   answer the phone
discuss marketing strategy

Administrative Staff	**Sales Staff**
	present new products

A VISIT TO A COMPANY

Daniel Carne is a client of Wyatt Ltd. Wyatt's public relations officer is giving him a tour of their main plant.

 Listen to the tape.
1. Say who he meets and which department they work in.
2. Mark (X) the job functions each person performs.

NAME	1	2	3	4
DEPT.				
TRAVEL				
TRAIN STAFF				
NEGOTIATE				
ATTEND MEETINGS				
PREPARE FIGURES				
SUPERVISE STAFF				

Check your information. Use the language box to help you.

Describing jobs

She is responsible for marketing.
She is in charge of administration.

He prepares figures.
He has to attend a lot of meetings.
She doesn't have to travel.

A JOB DESCRIPTION

Use your dictionary to find out about one or two of the jobs below. Ask someone else about the other jobs and make notes. Then give a brief description of them.

e.g. What does an architect do?   An architect designs buildings.

Maintenance Engineer
AUDITOR   Solicitor
Equity Manager   Copywriter
Medical Research Assistant
Tax Consultant   Civil Engineer
Air Traffic Controller
Public Relations Officer

INTRODUCING SOMEONE

Ask someone about his or her job and introduce him or her to a colleague. Use the language boxes to help you.

Finding out about jobs

What does your job involve?
What do you do in your job?

Do you have to/need to...?
Yes, I do./No, I don't.

Introductions

This is... She's a...
I'd like you to meet...

How do you do?
Pleased to meet you.

JOB PRIORITIES

Which of these are important to you? Number them from 1–8 (1 is the most important) and compare your list with another person.

Travel	Fringe benefits (company car, pension, etc.)
Responsibility	Opportunities for promotion
High salary	Long holidays
Job satisfaction	Meeting people

YOUR JOB

Which elements of your job do you like and why? Look at the language box to help you answer.

Likes and dislikes

He really likes
They like
You don't mind
I am not keen on

computers.
using computers.

Do you like making presentations?
Yes, I do./No, not really.

Common Errors

He has ~~have~~ to write reports.

What do you have ~~must you to~~ do?

Does he travel~~s~~ a lot?

Yes, I like it very much.

I don't mind working ~~to work~~ long hours.

CHECK YOUR GRAMMAR: PAGE 94.

JOB ADVERTISEMENTS   Look at these two job advertisements. Then write one for your own job.

Finance Manager
£25,000 plus

Icon Engineering requires a young, ambitious Financial Controller. Your responsibilities will involve cash flow, cost control, and budgeting. You will report to the Managing Director and take an active role in the planning and development of the company.

Experience of working in a busy office and handling computerized invoices is necessary. You must have at least three years experience, preferably with an engineering company.

Please send CV to:
Miss Sophie Watson
Icon Engineering
Burgstrasse 1
Zurich 32004
SWITZERLAND

Marketing
Executive
ATHENS
•
COMPANY CAR

Costas Scaltsas manufacture uPVC products for the building and electrical industry. We need a Marketing Executive to develop sales of our products in Eastern Europe.

The job involves market research, pricing strategy, PR, advertising, and publicity. Career opportunities are very good.

If you are interested, please telephone between 8 a.m. and 7 p.m. for more details, or send a CV and letter to our personnel manager, **Spiros Vlamakis** at:
COSTAS SCALTSAS
PIRAEUS
ATHENS
TELEPHONE: 301–743265
FAX: 301–743289

Costas Scaltsas

COMPANY ORGANIZATION

Look at the organization chart and use these job titles and company departments to complete it.

- Stores & Transport
- PRODUCTION DIRECTOR (VICE-PRESIDENT PRODUCTION)
- Export Sales Manager (Export Sales Director)
- Chief Accountant (Financial Controller)
- Health & Safety
- Advertising & Sales Promotion Manager (Advertising Director)

- MARKETING DIRECTOR (VICE-PRESIDENT MARKETING)
- Production Foreman
- Development Manager (Director R & D)
- Company Training Manager (Director of Training)

NOTE: (...) indicates American titles.

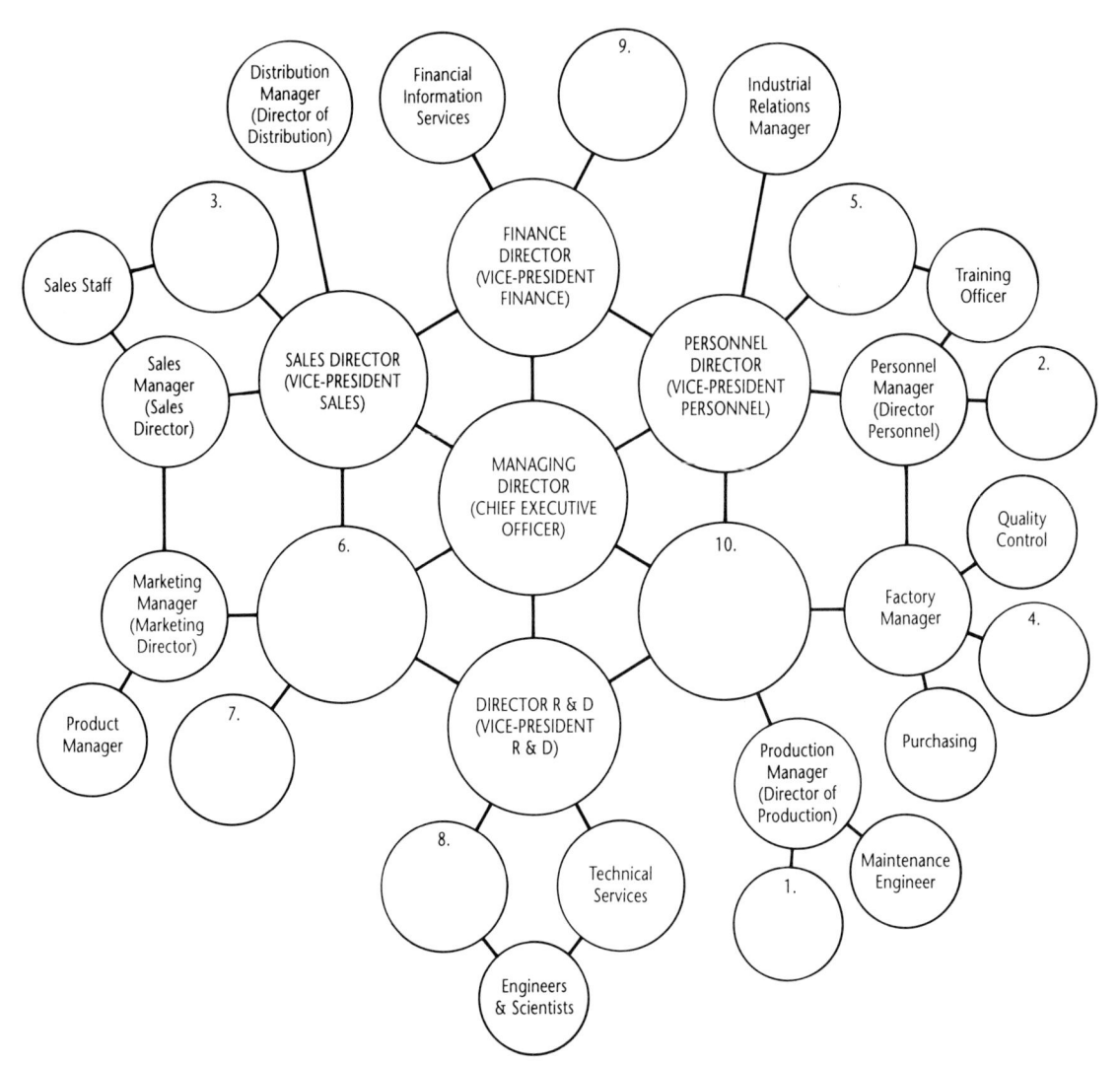

3   A BUSINESS TRIP

SPELLING

Complete the chart, putting letters which have the same sound together.

/eɪ/ as in day	A H _ _
/iː/ as in me	B C D _ _ _ _ _ (Z – American pronunciation)
/e/ as in pen	F L _ _ _ _ Z
/aɪ/ as in why	I _
/uː/ as in blue	Q _ _
/əʊ/ as in phone	O
/ɑː/ as in car	R

COMPANY NAMES

A stockbroker is talking on the phone to a client.

 Listen and write down the names of six multinationals and their annual turnover.

Name	Turnover (U.S. $bn)
Exxon	47.5

Look at one list of company names and spell three or four of them to someone else.

STUDENT A		**STUDENT B**	
Ferranti	Kirin	Speyhawk	Cemex
Losinger	Harima	Antifagosto	Pargesa
Framatome	Burns Fry	Kleinwort Charter	Orix

REQUESTING

Study these examples.

Could you order me a taxi?

Can you lend me a pen?

Could you possibly give me a lift to the airport?

Could I use your phone, please?

How you ask for something depends on:
- who you are talking to (stranger, client, colleague, etc.), and
- what you are asking for (a little or a lot).

 Listen to three short conversations and answer these questions.
1. Who is talking?
2. Where are they?
3. What are the three people asking for?

A BUSINESS TRIP

Your company, Energym, sells a range of fitness/exercise equipment. They are sending you to Hong Kong for a week. Here is a list of things you have to do before you leave. Choose words from the right to complete the list.

book	cancel
send	reserve
borrow	rent
lend	arrange
fix	find out
change	show
let someone know	

NOTES

Things to do

1 _____ taxi to the airport

2 _____ fax to agent in H.K.

3 _____ 2 tickets for opera on Friday

4 _____ names and addresses of possible contacts

5 _____ appointment with Robert Hurst

6 _____ street map of H.K. from Jerry

7 ____ Ken ____ time of arrival in H.K.

ASKING FOR HELP

You are now in Hong Kong. What would you say in these situations?

1. You would like to know the way to the Hyatt Regency Hotel. Ask someone.
2. You have no Hong Kong dollars, only U.S. dollars, and the banks are closed. Ask the hotel receptionist.
3. You would like a morning newspaper with your breakfast. Ask room service.
4. You would like to fax a message to your company but you have no time. Ask a secretary to do it.
5. A client is not sure if he will buy your product or not. You need to know his decision as soon as possible. Ask him.
6. You would like to have a look at a copy of your Hong Kong agent's new brochure. Ask her.
7. Your flight home is on Friday, but you want to stay in Hong Kong until Monday. Ask the travel agent.
8. A top client has invited you to play golf with him but you have no golf clubs. Ask a colleague for his clubs.

Now act out these situations. Use the language box to help you.

Requesting

Excuse me,...	Yes, of course.
Can you/Could you...?	I'm sorry, but...
Could I possibly...?	I'm afraid I...

FINDING OUT INFORMATION

While you are in Hong Kong you want to contact people who are interested in selling one of your new products, Exercycle 2000. You telephone the Hong Kong Chamber of Commerce for lists of fitness clubs and sports shops. Use the language box to help you.

STUDENT A

1. **Make the call:**

   Telephone the Hong Kong Chamber of Commerce and ask for the names and addresses of some fitness clubs.

2. **Receive the call:**

   You are the Hong Kong Chamber of Commerce. Here is a list of sports shops in Hong Kong.
   ● Intersport, 9 Hollywood Road
   ● Jansport, 30 Wing Lok Street
   ● Fila Cotton, 19 Hillier Street

STUDENT B

1. **Receive the call:**

   You are the Hong Kong Chamber of Commerce. Here is a list of fitness clubs in Hong Kong.
   ● Brannigan's, Tree Drive
   ● Pumping Iron, 48 Queen's Road
   ● J.C. Lee Centre, 14 Bonham Strand

2. **Make the call:**

   Telephone the Hong Kong Chamber of Commerce and ask for the names and addresses of some sports shops.

Checking information

Could you spell that?
How do you spell that?

Sorry?
Could you repeat that?

Common Errors

```
Can you to give me some information?
          lend
Can you borrow me...?
would
I like a...

Check:  g or j?  v or b?  i or e or a?
                 that
Could you repeat it?
```

CHECK YOUR GRAMMAR: PAGE 94/106.

A LETTER REQUESTING INFORMATION

Jochen Liesel sent two letters asking for information about a conference centre in Florida. The first was a letter to a friend and the second was a formal letter. Study the differences between them.

MEYER GmbH
IMBERGSTR. 46, 7000 STUTTGART 21

Bellevue Conference Center
1862 Sunset Boulevard
Fort Lauderdale
Florida FL 42000
U.S.A.

14 November

Ref: JL/npr/001

Dear Sirs,

We are planning to hold our annual conference in Florida in May next year and one of our clients, Matt Jessop, recommended Bellevue to us.

We would be grateful if you could send us a copy of your prospectus, details of accommodation, and a current price list.

We will require the facilities of the centre from 15 May for two weeks and expect approximately 150 delegates to attend.

We look forward to hearing from you.

Yours faithfully,

Jochen Liesel

JOCHEN LIESEL
Personnel

Meistersingerstr. 104
8000 Muenchen 81
Germany

17 October

Dear Matt,

I'm writing to ask you for your advice. We are looking for somewhere to hold our annual conference next year and I remember that you mentioned an excellent centre in Florida.

Could you possibly write and let me know the name of the centre and any other details which you think are useful? We need room for about 150 delegates for two weeks in May. I hope all this is not too inconvenient.

Regards to you and your family.

Yours,

Jochen

Now write a letter asking for information about a management training course. Write either to a friend who has experience of the course or to the company that runs the course.

PEOPLE AND BUILDINGS   Label the diagrams using the words below.

warehouse   staff/employees   retailer
office   management/executives   supplier
headquarters   board   wholesaler
factory/plant   manufacturer
subsidiary   importer
                                            consumer

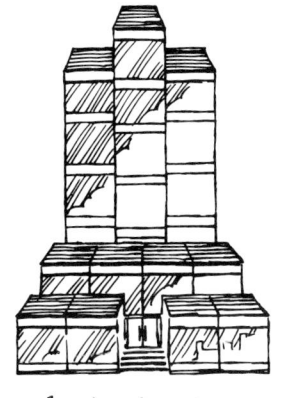

1   headquarters

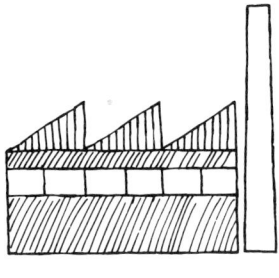

2

3

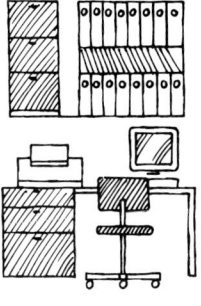

4

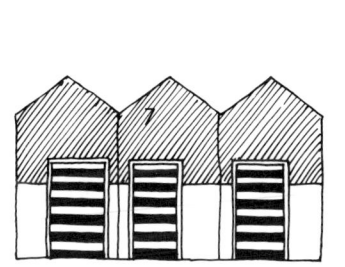

5

6

7

TRESTEL FRANCE
PART OF THE TRESTEL GROUP

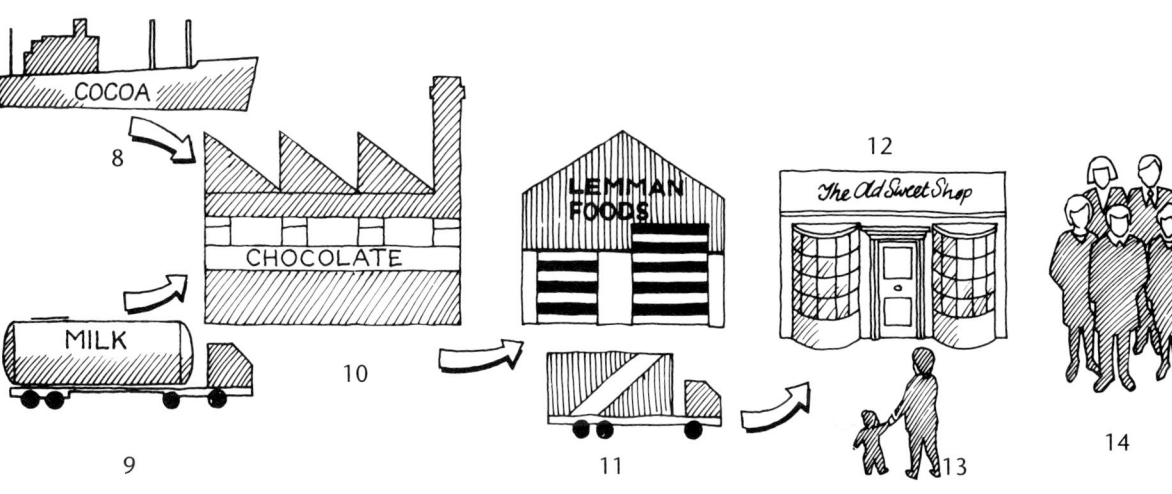

COCOA

8

CHOCOLATE

10

MILK

9

LEMMAN FOODS

11

The Old Sweet Shop

12

13

14

4   FACT FINDING

QUESTIONS

Complete the questions using the words below.

How long	Which	How often	When	What kind of
How far	What	How many	How much	

1. The hotel information desk

_____ restaurant is it?

_____ is it from here?

_____ time would you like to eat?

2. The Air Canada desk

_____ is the next flight to Vancouver?

_____ does it cost?

_____ flight would you like, the 8:20 or the 9:55?

3. A delivery firm

_____ boxes do you want to send?

_____ do you deliver to Georgetown?

_____ does it take?

 Now listen to the tape.

● Check your answers.

● Write down the answers to the questions.

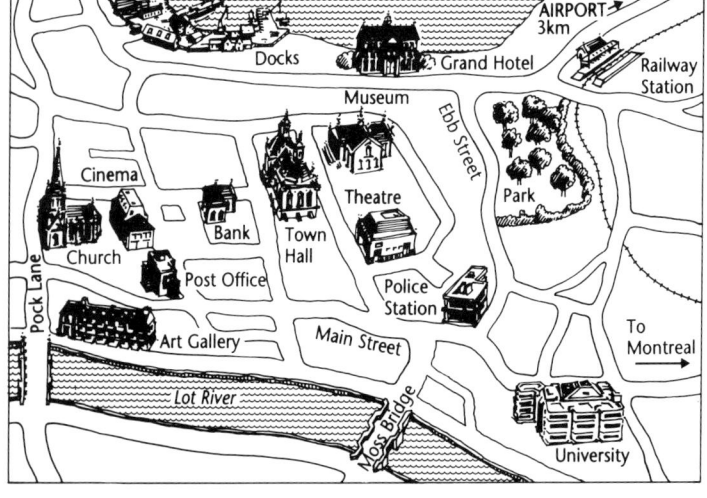

WHERE IS IT?

Look at the map and decide what **it** is in each sentence.

1. It's opposite the cinema.
2. It's behind the cinema.
3. It's near the river.
4. It's on the road to Montreal.
5. It's next to the cinema.
6. It's just past the park on the left.
7. It's outside the town.
8. It's on the corner of Main Street and Ebb Street.

FACT FINDING   Study the information about the Royal Hotel and Conference Center.

THE ROYAL HOTEL AND CONFERENCE CENTER

LOCATION:

The center is in Astoria, 50 miles from Seattle, and faces the Pacific Ocean.

TRANSPORT:

Special buses run from Seattle Airport to the center every two hours. There is also a local bus service.

HOTEL FACILITIES:

These include a swimming pool, sauna, tennis courts, bar, two restaurants, and a golf course 10 minutes away.

CONFERENCE FACILITIES:

Our conference room seats 280 people. There are also 8 large meeting rooms. We have all the necessary equipment, projectors, video, PA systems, and office support services (fax, photocopying, computing, and secretarial facilities).

EXCURSIONS:

There are trips to Vancouver Island, Montana, and the Rocky Mountains.

BOOKINGS:

We are open from March to December, but closed to conferences in August.

PRICES:

Hotel:
single room $54,
double room $87.

Conference center: prices on request.

Study the notes below and think about the questions you need to ask. Then talk to the other person.

STUDENT A

You are a conference centre manager in charge of bookings. Decide what kind of centre it is and what facilities it has. Ask the conference organizer for information about the conference (numbers, dates, etc.).

STUDENT B

You would like to organize a conference on marketing. Decide on the dates, numbers, and facilities you need. Ask the conference centre manager for information about the centre (accommodation, prices, transport to centre, etc.).

LISTEN AND SPEAK   A journalist who is interested in your company interviews you about your work. Listen to him and then reply. Keep your answers short and natural.

5 AN INVOICE FROM A SUPPLIER

DEALING WITH NUMBERS Look at these numbers.

108	one hundred and eight
2000	two thousand
643,218	six hundred and forty-three thousand, two hundred and eighteen
1001	one thousand and one
18,000,000	eighteen million
Tel: 010 221 42486	oh one oh double two one four two four eight six
1.5 kg	one point five kilos
0.005 mm	point oh oh five of a millimetre
27.27	twenty-seven point two seven
1/2 l	half a litre
£750,000	three-quarters of a million pounds
28%	twenty-eight percent
1:20	one in twenty
3 x 4 m	three metres by four metres
$2.40	two dollars forty cents
¥250	two hundred and fifty yen

1/2	a half	1/3	a third	1/4	a quarter
1/5	a fifth	1/8	an eighth	1/10	a tenth
2/3	two-thirds	3/4	three-quarters	5/8	five-eighths

+ plus	- minus	÷ divided by	x times

Now say these.

7000	0.336	60%	3 x 8 x 12 m
$11.80	3/8	740,188	Tel: 720 4413

Listen and check

FACT FILE

Spanish Industrial Clothing (SIC) is a company which produces protective clothing – gloves, overalls, masks, etc. – for industrial use.

Listen to the information about the company and fill in the figures.

Company name: Spanish Industrial Clothing (SIC)
Nearest city:
Range of products:
Share of home market:
Turnover:
Exports:
Workforce – total:
           women:

ORDERING SUPPLIES

Duroglas is a bottling plant at Hendaye in France. Its employees have to wear special clothing at work.

Monique Martin, purchasing manager at Duroglas, needs to purchase new supplies of gloves and overalls for the factory workers. She usually buys these in bulk from SIC.

Listen to her phone conversation and complete the order form below.

ORDER FORM

GLOVES

Type	Size	Unit Price	Quantity
AG 3	8	175	
	10	175	
	12	185	
AG 7	8	200	
	10	200	
	12	200	
RG 7	8		100
	10		
	TOTAL:		

OVERALLS

Colour	Size	Unit Price	Quantity
Grey	Small	2000	
	Medium	2200	
	Large	2400	20
Light Blue	Small		
	Medium		10
	Large		
		TOTAL:	

5 AN INVOICE FROM A SUPPLIER

PLACING AN ORDER

Here are ten steps in ordering goods. The ones on the left are for the purchaser, the ones on the right for the supplier. Put them in the correct order (1–10).

<u>2</u> Telephone the supplier   — Dispatch the goods

— Sign the delivery note   — Pass the order on to the store

— Check the goods on arrival   manager

<u>1</u> Do a stock check   — Deliver the goods

— Place an order   — Fill out an order form

     — Make up the order

Now say what happened with the order which Monique Martin placed with SIC. Begin like this: "Monique did a stock check. Then she telephoned SIC and..."

PRONUNCIATION

The past tense ending **-ed** produces three different sounds:
/t/   as in passed
/d/   as in delivered
/ɪd/   as in needed (only with words ending **-ted** or **-ded)**

Say these.

wanted	used	ordered	stopped	called
returned	contacted	asked	decided	arrived
purchased	prepared			

 Now listen and check.

WHAT WENT WRONG?

When they unpacked the goods, Duroglas discovered that there was a mistake. Suggest what went wrong.

e.g. (fill out)   Perhaps they did not fill out the order form correctly.

1. (make up)
2. (dispatch)
3. (check)

CHECK YOUR GRAMMAR: PAGE 88.

AN INVOICE FROM A SUPPLIER

STUDENT A

You are Monique Martin. You receive this invoice from SIC. Look at the invoice and the order form and telephone Nuria at SIC to tell her about the mistakes. Use the language boxes to help you.

STUDENT B

You are Nuria at SIC. You receive a call from Monique Martin. Look at the invoice and correct it when she tells you about the mistakes. Use the language boxes to help you.

SPANISH INDUSTRIAL CLOTHING

INVOICE

DELIVERY ADDRESS

Duroglas S.A.
Zone Industrielle
Hendaye
France

Invoice Date	Account Number	Invoice Number (Please quote in all correspondence)			
QUANTITY	DESCRIPTION	List Price	Gross	Discount %	Net
	GLOVES				
100	AG7 Size 10	200	20,000	10%	18,000
150	AG7 Size 12	200	30,000	10%	27,000
100	RG7 Size 8	250	25,000	10%	22,500
100	RG7 Size 10	250	25,000	10%	22,500
	OVERALLS				
30	Grey: Medium	2200	66,000	10%	59,400
20	Large	2400	48,000	10%	43,200
20	Light blue: Small	2000	40,000	10%	36,000
30	Medium	2200	66,000	10%	59,400
		Total Goods	Total Discount		Invoice Total
		Pta 320,000	Pta 32,000		Pta 288,000

Correcting information

I ordered... but you sent...
I didn't want... I wanted...

Not TWENty-two, but THIRty-two.

You sent us the wrong.../too many...

You didn't send enough...

Checking facts and reacting

What was that again?
Did you say TWENty-two?

So, that's...

I see.
Fine.
I'm sorry about that.

Common Errors

He wanted two thousands.

They stole eighteen millions.

He did not arrived.

Did you wanted...?
did
I not ordered...

enough
I don't have ~~so much~~ money.

It's too ~~much~~ expensive.

Use the information below to find answers to the questions.

GSA WATER PURIFIERS

Our purifiers are unique because they contain a carbon filter which is impregnated silver. Silver stops the growth of bacteria inside the unit. The results of a government test show how GSA products compare with ordinary water filters.

GSA 200T

- economical
- no installation necessary
- cleaner water from your tap

Height 280 mm

Width 100 mm

Weight 3.2 kg

Capacity 50,000 l

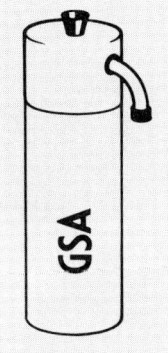

GSA 500T

- large capacity
- professional installation recommended
- cleans all the water you use

Height 410 mm

Width 150 mm

Weight 15.4 kg

Capacity 290,000 l

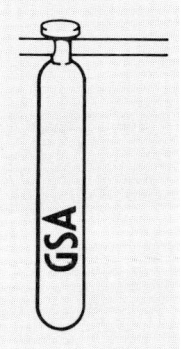

GSA 10D

- portable
- lightweight
- good for travel, camping, etc.

Height 150 mm

Width 80 mm

Weight 0.5 kg

Capacity 1800 l

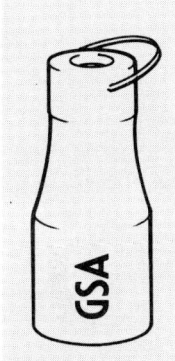

Test TN1 (After passing 1000 litres through the unit)

Unit	Organisms introduced	Organisms after treatment
GSA 200T	600	3
GSA 500T	600	1
GSA 10D	300	5
Ordinary filter 1	300	740
Ordinary filter 2	600	3010

1. What is the main selling point of the GSA 200T?
2. There is one unit which you cannot put in yourself. Which one?
3. The GSA 10D is the same size as:

    a) a bottle of wine   b) a jar of marmalade   c) a tube of toothpaste
4. What is the problem with ordinary filters?

DATES AND TIMES

Study these.

first, second, third, fourth, fifth, sixth, seventh, etc.

27 September	the twenty-seventh of September
1 April	the first of April
15/2/94	the fifteenth of February, nineteen ninety-four
5/7/88	the fifth of July, nineteen eighty-eight or, in the U.S.A., May seventh nineteen eighty-eight

three o'clock

half past seven or seven-thirty

quarter past (U.S. – after) five
or five-fifteen

quarter to four or
three forty-five

ten past (U.S. – after) two
or two-ten

twenty-five to ten
or nine thirty-five

3 p.m.	three o'clock in the afternoon
8:15 a.m.	eight-fifteen in the morning

AT	6 o'clock, twenty past nine, lunchtime, night, the weekend, the beginning/end of the year/month etc., Christmas/Easter etc.
ON	Tuesday, 12 October, the first day of the course
IN	June, 1999, the spring/winter etc., the morning/afternoon/evening.

Now answer these questions. When:

...were you born?   ...do you have your main meal?
...do you get up?   ...is your next national holiday?
...do you arrive at work?   ...does the financial year end in your country?

A SITUATION REPORT

INVESTING IN PROPERTY

Your company wants to buy a hotel in this area. These two hotels are for sale. Say which you think is the better investment. Use the language box to help you.

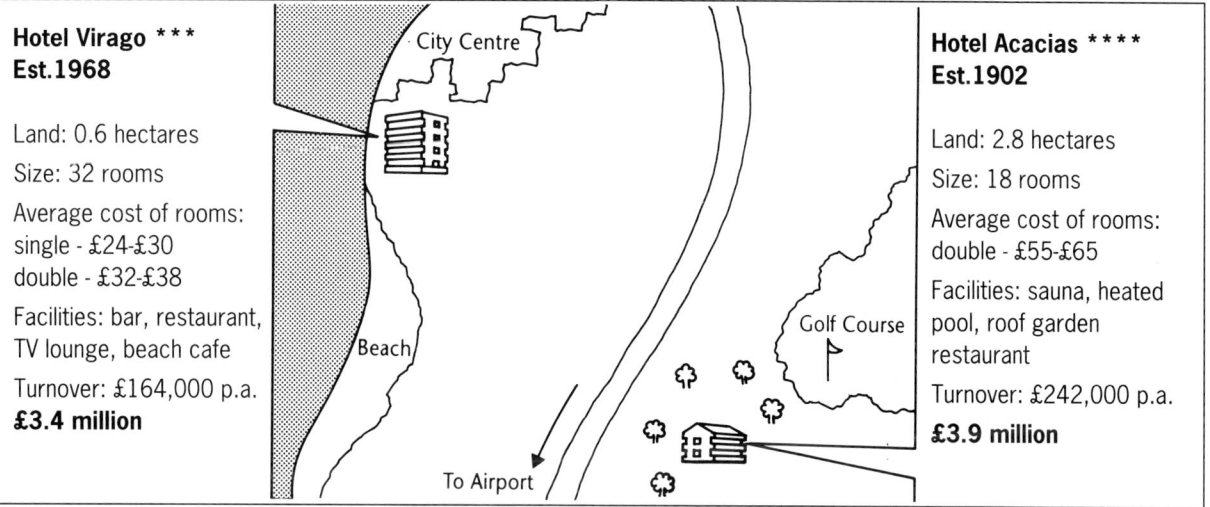

Hotel Virago ★ ★ ★
Est.1968

Land: 0.6 hectares

Size: 32 rooms

Average cost of rooms:
single - £24-£30
double - £32-£38

Facilities: bar, restaurant, TV lounge, beach cafe

Turnover: £164,000 p.a.
£3.4 million

City Centre

Beach

To Airport

Golf Course

Hotel Acacias ★ ★ ★ ★
Est.1902

Land: 2.8 hectares

Size: 18 rooms

Average cost of rooms:
double - £55-£65

Facilities: sauna, heated pool, roof garden restaurant

Turnover: £242,000 p.a.
£3.9 million

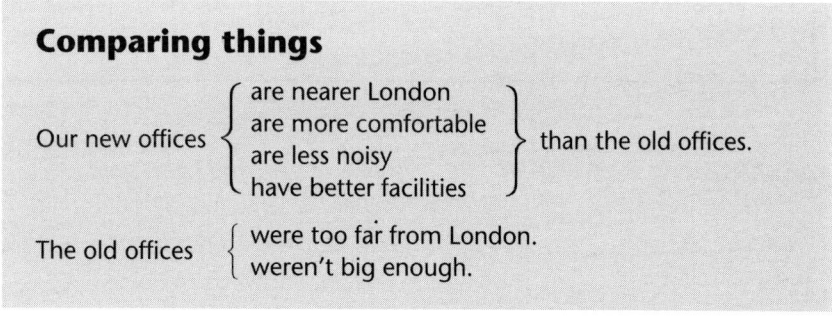

Comparing things

| Our new offices | { are nearer London / are more comfortable / are less noisy / have better facilities } | than the old offices. |

| The old offices | { were too far from London. / weren't big enough. } |

CHECK YOUR GRAMMAR: PAGE 99.

MARKET TRENDS

Six months ago, a travel magazine published a report on trends in the holiday market. Read the report on the next page and complete the chart. Check the meaning of these words first.

package holiday   abroad   resort   tour operator

Holidays – the way forward?

70% of Europeans who go abroad for their holidays book package holidays at resorts on the Mediterranean coast, in countries like Spain, Portugal, Turkey, and Greece. The number of these resorts is increasing all the time and developers are continuing to buy up land for new hotels and apartments.

But more and more people are trying to find a different kind of holiday, away from the crowds. They are travelling longer distances to places like Thailand or Florida. Others, especially in the 40–60 age group, are taking their holidays in the low season, at quieter times of the year. But the majority of Europeans still prefer to travel in July and August.

A major problem for tour operators is how to give customers the security of a well-organized holiday, and at the same time, the independence they want – a holiday experience that is personal and unique.

One solution is special interest holidays. These are becoming more popular, especially with American visitors to Europe. Thousands visit France each year for wine-tasting in the Bordeaux region or riding and canoeing in the Dordogne.

The Holiday Market

General Description

1. 70% book package holidays at Mediterranean resorts.

2. The majority take holidays in July and August.

3. Thousands visit France each year on special interest holidays.

Trends

1. The number of holiday resorts is increasing.

2. _____

3. _____

4. _____

5. _____

6. _____

DESCRIBING A MARKET

Choose a market you know well.
- Prepare a general description of it.
- Give details of trends in it.

Use the language box to help you.

Describing markets

The market for mobile homes is quite small/competitive.
The majority of people stay in hotels.
Last year British companies sold over 20,000 mobile homes.

Describing trends

More people are buying mobile homes.
The demand for mobile homes is increasing.
More and more companies are entering the market.

A SITUATION REPORT   Ronald de Raad works for a Dutch tour operator, Valken N.V. He is in charge of their cycling holidays in Sardinia. He telephones Anna Martelli, the area co-ordinator, to report on the situation.

    Listen to his telephone conversation.
- Mark (X) the problems he mentions.
- Write down what he is doing about each one.

PROBLEM	ACTION HE IS TAKING
1. DELAY IN DELIVERY OF BICYCLES	_____
2. FOREST FIRE	_____
3. AIRPORT IS CLOSED	_____
4. CUSTOMERS ARE UNHAPPY	_____
5. HOTEL IS OVERBOOKED	_____

CHECK YOUR GRAMMAR: PAGE 84.

DEALING WITH PROBLEMS   You are Ronald de Raad in Sardinia. Look at these problems and telephone Anna Martelli to say what you are doing about each one.

1. The airport is closed.
2. A hotel which the company always uses is overbooked and cannot accommodate your customers.
3. One of your tour leaders left her job yesterday, before the end of the tour.
4. Three of your customers are very ill after eating fish in a hotel.

A MEMO

Look at this memo which Anna Martelli sent to her boss at Valken's head office in Rotterdam about the situation in Sardinia.

Valken N.V.

INTERNAL MEMO

To: Hub Kessels, Rotterdam   **Date:**   12 August
From: Anna Martelli, Italy   **Subject:** Sardinian Tours

As you know, there is a fire in Sardinia. Luckily everyone is O.K. and Ronnie, our courier, has the situation under control. Some customers are now in hotels in Cagliari, others are flying home. We are cancelling all bookings for next week.

Using one of the other problems, write another memo to head office.

Common Errors

                    getting
The situation is ~~get~~ worse.
        produces
IBM ~~is producing~~ computers.

Turkey is ~~more~~ cheaper than France.
                        than
Our company charges less ~~that~~ others.
    people
More ~~persons~~ are buying our products.

Read the memo and then answer the questions below.

Lawson Educational Books

MEMO

Subject: Trip to Far East   From: J. Francis (Area Manager)
Date: 22/1   To: D. Swain (Sales Manager)

TAIWAN

The signs for this year and next year are good. The government is building four new universities and is increasing library budgets by 15%.

TAIPEI BOOKFAIR: This was the main reason for my visit. Our display of 800 books looked good and I had some useful discussions with importers. Our main competitor - Heinemann - was not present.

NEEDS: One problem, as business increases, is the language barrier. At the moment we are using an interpreter, but we really need an English-speaking consultant to work with us here.

We need to get more information to the end-users to increase the demand for our books. I think now is the time to start distributing more catalogues.

1. Who is the main competitor of: a) Lawson Books? b) your company?
2. Who are the end-users of: a) Lawson's products? b) your company's products?
3. What is the way to increase the demand for: a) Lawson's books? b) your company's products?

ADJECTIVES AND NOUNS

Some words naturally go together. When you learn a new word, it is also useful to learn the words that go with it.

e.g. to arrive **in** or **at** (*not* arrive to)
a **high** price (*not* a big price)

Look at the list of nouns and choose adjectives that go with them.

useful, brief, serious	discussion	_____	loss
_____	meeting	_____	event
_____	idea	_____	meal
_____	report	_____	man
_____	decision	_____	car
_____	problem	_____	factory
_____	price	_____	country

quick	nice	young	serious	high
fast	kind	modern	heavy	large
brief	useful	recent	important	tall
	good			

7   ENTERTAINING A CLIENT

EXPLAINING THE MENU   Fill in the menu with a few of your favourite dishes from around the world or with specialities from your region. Then describe each dish, using the language box and a dictionary to help you.

Menu

Starters

Main Courses

Desserts

Service not included

Describing food

What is (in) the Sambal?
How is it cooked?

It is a local speciality.
It is made with...
It's a kind of soup/stew/vegetable.

It's quite hot/spicy/salty/rich/filling.
It's a sweet/savoury dish.
It's baked/boiled/fried.

I (don't) think you'll like it.

ENTERTAINING A CLIENT

Lisa Erikson is on business in Indonesia. Her company's agent in Jakarta, Halima Hassan, invites her for dinner at a local restaurant. Decide who says the following.

Can I take your order now?	I recommend the Satay.
It's a little too sweet for me.	The bill, please. ('check' in U.S.
Is everything O.K.?	English)
Please. I'll get this./This is on me.	What would you like to drink?
Do any vegetables come with it?	Enjoy your meal.
Is it hot?	Do you have a reservation?
Would you like a starter?	I'll have the Satay.
Can you tell me what is in the Satay?	More wine?
How is your Satay?	A table for two, please.

Waiter	Halima	Lisa
Can I take your order now?		

Put the phrases above into order. Using a menu, role play a conversation between a waiter and two customers.

LISTEN AND SPEAK

You are visiting the Middle East on business.

Listen to the speaker in each situation and then reply. Keep your answers short and natural.

- At the airport
- At the hotel
- Buying a film

AN IMPORTANT MESSAGE

GETTING THROUGH

Look at these phrases and decide which person says each one.

e.g. I'd like to speak to Mrs Cameron.

I'd like to speak to Mrs Cameron.
Yes, speaking.
Can I speak to someone who deals with...?
Who's calling, please?
Could I have the sales department, please?
Hold the line, please.
Sorry. You have the wrong number.
No thanks. I'll call back later.
My name is...

One moment. I'll put you through.
Hello. Sales.
I'm inquiring about...
Leo Wan here. Can I help you?
The line's busy. Will you hold?
Is that Leo Wan's office?
Knox Oil and Gas. Good afternoon.
Can I tell her who called?
Sorry. You have the wrong extension.

Caller

Switchboard

Receiver

Look at these four conversations.

● Decide what you think the caller said.

 ● Listen to the tape and compare your answers with what you hear.

1. B Hello. Argus Engineering.
   A _____
   B Mr. Franks? Just a moment... I'm sorry, the line's busy. Will you hold?
   A _____
   B Can I tell him who called?
   A _____
   B Right, Mr Carey. I'll tell him you called.

2. B Gamble and Proud. Good morning.
   A _____
   B I'm sorry. Which department?
   A _____
   B Just a moment. I'll put you through.
   C Personnel.
   A _____
   C Hold the line. I'll get him for you.
   D Hello. Robert Turner here.

3. B Hello. Japan Airlines.
   A _____
   B One moment. I'll put you through to the booking desk.
   C International flights. Can I help you?
   A _____
   C Certainly, sir. When would you like to travel?

4. B Hello. Cale and Cale, Solicitors.
   A _____
   B Yes, speaking.
   A _____
   B I'm sorry. I'm busy on Friday. Is Thursday possible for you?

WILL AND -'LL

Look at the examples and then reply to the other sentences using **will** or -'ll.

e.g. Sorry, the line's busy.   (Quick decision) I'll phone back later.

I'd like to speak to the manager.   (Offer) I'll get him for you.

1. I'm really thirsty.   (Offer)
2. Sorry, sir. There's no fish on the menu today.   (Quick decision)
3. This is the report for Dave Butz.   (Offer)
4. This one is $32 and that one is $48.   (Quick decision)
5. AMC want an answer from you soon.   (Quick decision)
6. Mr Chiu wants to go to the theatre while he's here.   (Offer)

CHECK YOUR GRAMMAR: PAGE 86.

ON THE PHONE

You are going to make a number of short phone calls to different people. Listen to the first two examples before you try them yourself and then try the others. Look at the instructions before each one.

1. You are phoning: Delhi Railway Station.
   Reason for call: You want to know the times of trains to Calcutta this afternoon.

2. You are phoning: NBK Air Conditioning Systems, sales department.
   Reason for call: You want to order a system for an office 30 m x 50 m x 3 m.

3. You are phoning: The Taj Mahal Restaurant.
   Reason for call: You want to book a table for four for tonight.

4. You are phoning: Kline Ferguson Inc.
   Reason for call: You want to speak to Jeff Gomez.

5. You are phoning: The Surrey Post (newspaper), advertising department.
   Reason for call: You want to place an advertisement in the business-to-business column.

6. You are phoning: Allied Webb Financial Services.
   Reason for call: You want to know about their U.S. investment fund. Ask them to send you a brochure.

AN IMPORTANT MESSAGE Look at your instructions. Prepare to make two calls and to receive two calls. Write down any messages. Use the language box to help you.

STUDENT A

Make calls 1 & 2:

1. You are John Wyatt. You want to cancel your appointment at 3 p.m. tomorrow with Roberta Hunt, the customer services manager. Ask her if 4 p.m. next Tuesday is possible.

2. You manage the cosmetics department at B & A department store. You have two new sales assistants who need some training. Telephone the customer services manager at Benito to ask for her help.

Receive calls 3 & 4:

You work for Mackeson Property U.K. in the accounts department. The chief accountant, Mr Side, is on holiday for a week. Take any messages for him.

STUDENT B

Receive calls 1 & 2:

You work in the customer services department of Benito Cosmetics. Your manager, Roberta Hunt, is out of the office today. Take any messages for her.

Make calls 3 & 4:

3. Your company, Ellis & Co., did some building work for Mackeson Property U.K. four months ago. You are still waiting for payment. Call their chief accountant.

4. You are Anna Ferndale from the head office of Mackeson Property U.K. You want the sales figures for last January. Call Mr Side in the accounts department.

Telephone call for _____

Caller's name _____

Caller's number _____

Message

Taken by: _____

Telephone call for _____

Caller's name _____

Caller's number _____

Message

Taken by: _____

Giving and receiving messages

Can you give him a message?

I'm sorry. He's not here at the moment.
Sorry, his line's busy.
Can I help?
Can I take a message?

I'll give him your message.
I'll ask her to call you.

Common Errors

I want ~~that~~ *him to* ~~he~~ call me.

Could you *tell* ~~say to~~ him to call me?

I'll get ~~I get~~ him for you.

Hello. ~~Here is~~ Peter Wright *speaking*.

Label the pictures with words from the text.

Telecommunications

There has been a revolution in telecommunications over the past 20 years: the radio phone, the fax (facsimile) machine, and the answer phone are now part of our daily lives. In the 1990's we can expect development in two main areas.

1 Information services

The user plugs a keyboard and screen into his telephone. He can then find out how much money he has in the bank, order an armchair from a shop, or see the menu of a local Chinese restaurant.

2 The use of radio phones

In many places, public telephones are now difficult to find. The Phonepoint is one alternative. The user has a portable handset. If he wants to make a phone call, he only needs to stand near a Phonepoint transmitter (200 metres or less).

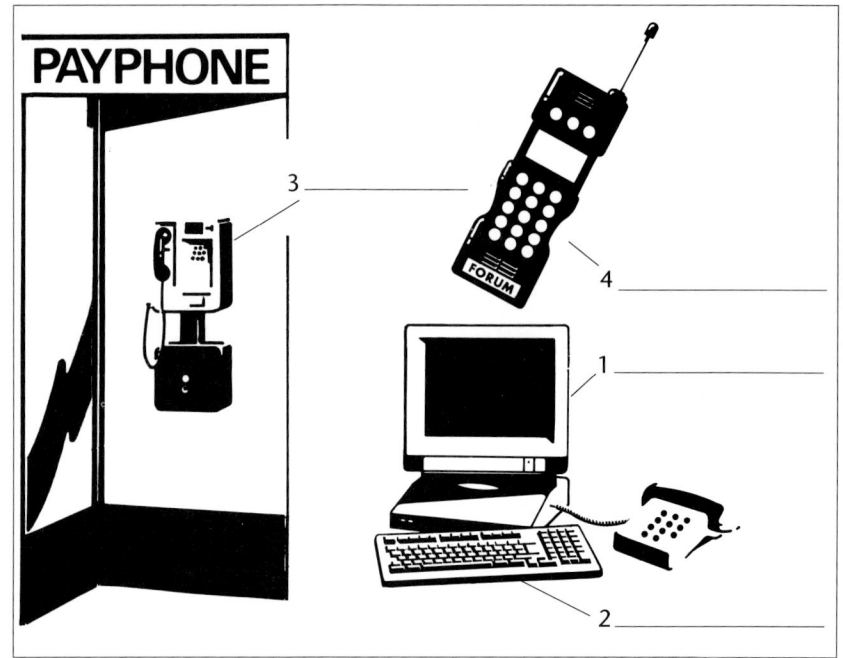

PAYPHONE

3 _____

4 _____

1 _____

2 _____

MONEY

Put each pair or group of words into the correct sentence. Make sure you use the correct form.

profit	bill ('check' in U.S. English)	to cost	to invest
loss	invoice	to be worth	to save

salary	to spend	charge	to waste	to pay back
wage	to earn	price	to save	to owe
				to afford

e.g. _Profits_ were good last year, but this year I think we are going to make a _loss_ .

1. I have got $6000. I can either _____ it on the stock market or I can _____ it for my next holiday.
2. He never has any money because he _____ more than he _____.
3. The company plans to increase the _____ of factory personnel by 10%. Directors' _____ will only go up by 4%.
4. Please pay your hotel and restaurant _____ now and you can send us an _____ for all your expenses at the end of the trip.
5. The car _____ £5000 in 1989 but now it _____ only £600.
6. I must _____ the $1200 that I _____ to the bank. I can't _____ the interest.
7. Don't _____ your money on a train ticket. You can _____ £6, if you go by bus.
8. There is no extra _____ for delivery; it's included in the _____.

A LOOK AT THE FIGURES

DESCRIBING PERFORMANCE

Look at the verbs and match them with the right headlines.

go (went) up
improve (improved)
drop (dropped)
remain (remained) at that level

stand (stood) at
go (went) down
rise (rose)

increase (increased)
stay (stayed) the same
be (was/were)
fall (fell)

Daily News
OUTPUT UP

1.

Daily News
INFLATION DOWN

2.

Daily News
EXPORTS £50 MILLION

3.

Daily News
UNEMPLOYMENT: NO CHANGE

4.

e.g. Output went up

Here is some information about three European pharmaceutical manufacturers. Use the words above to describe their performance between 1986 and 1990.

e.g. RP's share of the market fell by 4% to 20%.

European Pharmaceutical Market

Market share

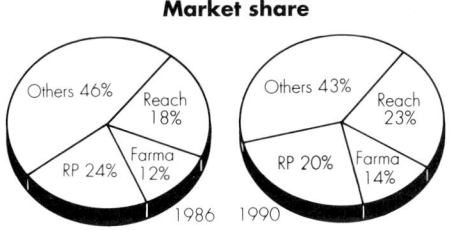

Others 46% / Reach 18% / Farma 12% / RP 24%
1986

Others 43% / Reach 23% / Farma 14% / RP 20%
1990

Capital expenditure on land, buildings, plant, and equipment 1986–1990

	(£ millions)	
---	1986	1990
Farma	11.6	13.9
RP	14.8	13.2
Reach	8.7	10.9

Annual R & D Expenditure

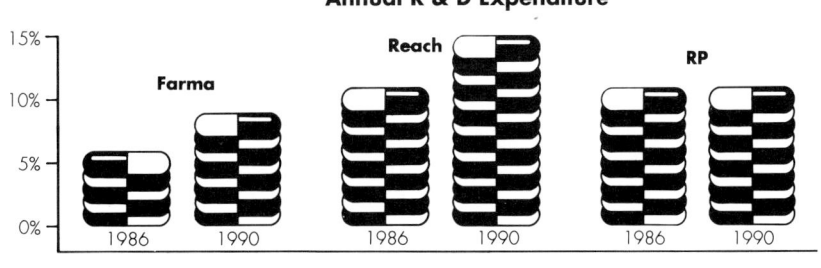

9 A LOOK AT THE FIGURES

DESCRIBING A GRAPH   Look at the graph and use these words to complete the sentences.

at the end of	until	slowly
at the beginning of	over	rapidly
between...and...	in	sharply
		slightly

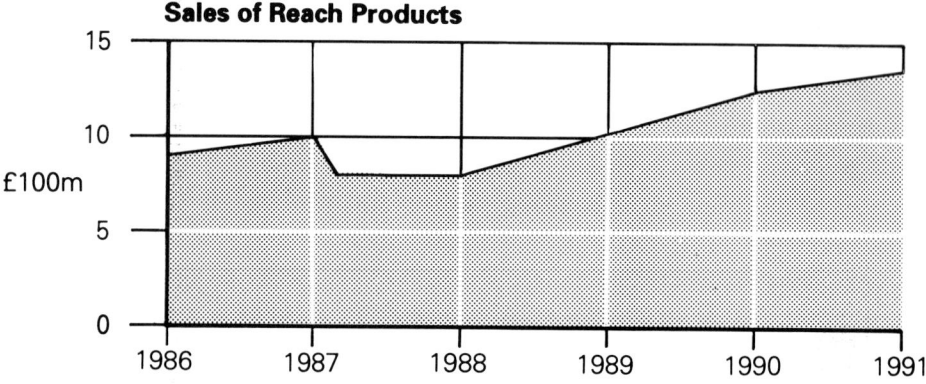

Sales of Reach Products

1. _____ January 1986, sales stood at £900 million.
2. _____ the next 12 months they rose _____.
3. But _____ 1987 they dropped _____ to £700 million.
4. They remained at this level _____ the end of 1987.
5. _____ 1988 _____ 1990 they increased _____ and reached £1,250 million.
6. In 1990 they continued to rise, but more _____ and _____ 1990 sales were £1,380 million.

A SALES REPORT   Read the report about the first year's sales of the antibiotic Trioxil.

Reach Pharmaceuticals S.A.

Sales of Trioxil 1990 – 91

In August 1989 we launched a new antibiotic, Trioxil. In 1990 sales of the new product increased rapidly worldwide and today stand at over 130 million Swiss Francs.

In Japan sales were slow at the beginning of the year because we had problems with distribution. In May we reached an agreement with a new distributor and the situation improved. Sales over the year rose by 24% to 18.6 million Swiss Francs.

In the more competitive U.S. market, sales stayed at their 1989 level due to a sharp fall in the value of the dollar.

In 1989 Junior Delpol was the best selling children's antibiotic in the world. But European sales of the product dropped slightly. So, in August 1990 we launched Junior Trioxil in Italy. In its first six months sales reached 5.4 million Swiss Francs.

Make questions about the report to go with the answers below.

e.g. When was Trioxil launched?   In August 1989.

1. Why _____?   Because of distribution problems.
2. When _____?   When they reached an agreement with a new distributor.
3. Why _____?   Due to a fall in the value of the dollar.
4. What _____?   Junior Delpol.
5. Why _____?   Because European sales of Junior Delpol dropped in 1989.

CHECK YOUR GRAMMAR: PAGE 88.

A LOOK AT THE FIGURES   Every year at the Healthcare Exhibition in Switzerland manufacturers of medical equipment show their new products to customers from all over the world. The two bar charts below give information about the number of exhibitors and the number of visitors.

Listen to Kristina Rufli as she explains the bar charts.
- Find the reasons she gives for the changes A, B, C, D.
- Explain the figures in each chart using the language box to help you.

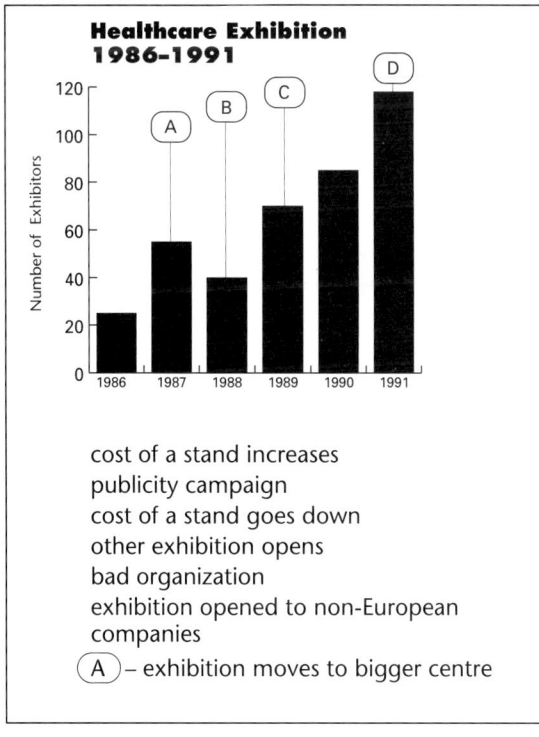

Healthcare Exhibition 1986-1991

cost of a stand increases
publicity campaign
cost of a stand goes down
other exhibition opens
bad organization
exhibition opened to non-European companies
(A) – exhibition moves to bigger centre

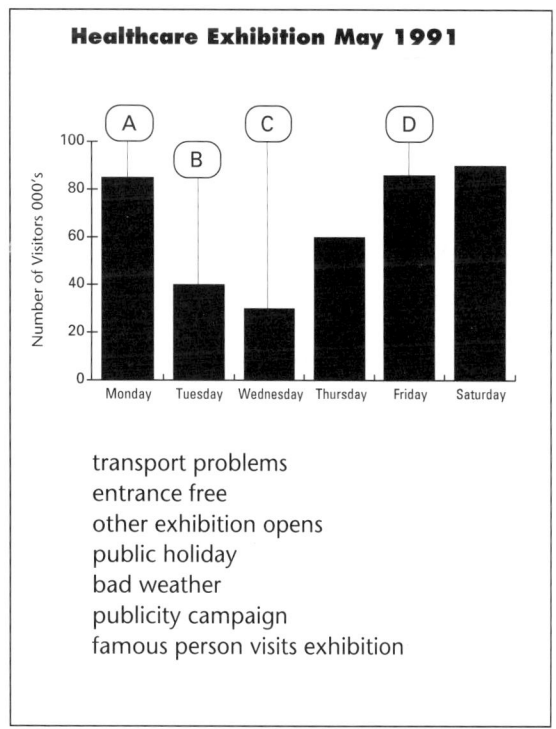

Healthcare Exhibition May 1991

transport problems
entrance free
other exhibition opens
public holiday
bad weather
publicity campaign
famous person visits exhibition

Explaining figures

Numbers fell due to/because of bad publicity.

Sales rose because it was Christmas time.

The situation improved when we opened a new office in Milan.

Prepare a short presentation of a graph or chart about:
1. Your company (past performance).
2. Sales of a product you know well.
3. The European pharmaceuticals market.

Common Errors

Production of cars fell ~~down~~ in 1990.

In
~~On~~ January 1990...

1989 ~~it~~ was a good year for us.

did   *rise*
Why ~~rose~~ unemployment?

Study this campaign plan and then devise one yourself for a product you know well.

DELTA PLASTIC LAMINATES LTD

CAMPAIGN PLAN

Product: Electronic laminates

Customers: Electronics industry for use in telephones, computers, hi-fi equipment, aircraft control, etc.

Aims: To promote – our customer services and technical support
                     – an image of product quality and reliability

Campaign:
1. Direct mail to selected customers
2. Feature articles on products and company in technical journals/magazines
3. News reports of new contracts in business press
4. Presentation of products to customers
5. Displays at exhibitions and trade fairs

SALES AND MARKETING

Choose a word from the right to go with the words on the left.

a sales	_____	campaign
a special	_____	research
a competitive	_____	target
market	_____	offer
a product	_____	outlet
an advertising	_____	market
a major	_____	competitor
an up-market	_____	range
a retail	_____	image
a brand	_____	name

Now say three things about your company's products and how they are marketed.

10 SAYING THE RIGHT THING

SHORT ANSWERS

When someone asks you a question it is not always polite to answer only "yes" or "no". A short answer like "yes, I am" or "no, it isn't" is often more natural or friendly. For questions 1–6, find the correct answer. Then make short answers for the other questions.

1. Are you married?	No, I don't.
2. Is it very far?	Yes, he does.
3. Do you work for RBC?	Yes, it was.
4. Does Pierre live in Toulon?	No, it isn't.
5. Was the meeting useful?	No, I didn't.
6. Did you see Max yesterday?	Yes, I am.
7. Did John leave a message?	_____
8. Am I speaking too fast for you?	_____
9. Does it cost a lot?	_____
10. Were their prices too high?	_____
11. Is English a difficult language?	_____
12. Are they here?	_____

SAYING THE RIGHT THING

Study the short responses below and then use them to complete the dialogue.

Someone says	You say	Someone says	You say
I...	Really?	Can I...?	Certainly.
	I see.		Of course.
	Congratulations!		Please do.
	I'm sorry to hear that.		Sorry, but...
e.g. I work for the government.	I see.	e.g. Can I use your phone?	Of course.

Someone says	**You say**	**Someone says**	**You say**
Would you like...?	Yes, please. No, thanks. That's very kind of you.	I'm afraid...	That's all right./O.K. Never mind. Don't worry.
e.g. Would you like a map?	Yes, please.	e.g. I'm afraid I don't know the address.	Never mind.

Someone says	**You say**
Is/are...?	Yes, that's right. I (don't) think so. I'm not sure. Well no, actually. I'm afraid not. I hope so.

e.g. Is he in his office?   I don't think so.

You are on a business trip in Prague. You are sitting in the garden of your hotel, reading a book. A man speaks to you. Answer him, keeping your answers short and natural.

He says	You say
Excuse me. Can I sit here?	e.g. Yes. Please do.
It's a beautiful evening, isn't it?	
I see you are reading a German book. Are you from Germany?	
Really? Where are you from exactly?	
I know it well. I was there only last year.	
Oh, it was fantastic. I was on holiday with my family for two weeks. We wanted to stay longer, but my wife was ill and we had to come back.	
Oh, she's fine now. Are you on holiday here?	
And you're staying at this hotel?	
Can I get you a drink? I'm going to have one.	
Sorry, I couldn't get a drink. The bar's closed.	
Would you like coffee instead?	
So...is it your first visit here?	
Will there be any more in the future?	
Well, I hope so. Prague is a beautiful city.	
Well...will you excuse me? I need to make a phone call. Do you know if there is a public telephone in the hotel?	
O.K. See you again, perhaps.	

Now act out a similar conversation.

LISTEN AND SPEAK   You arrive in the U.S.A. to visit your agent, Mike Bukowski.

Listen to the speaker in each situation and then reply. Keep your answers short and natural.

- At passport control
- Telephoning Mike Bukowski
- At lunch

11 A MANUFACTURING PROCESS

INSTRUCTIONS

— jack

wheel nuts

receipts

Here are some notes on how to do three things. Put the notes into the right order and then use the language box to help you explain each operation. Begin like this: "First insert the card. Then..."

1. Getting cash from an automatic dispenser
- Key in your personal number
- Take your cash
- Wait for the machine to check your number
- Remove the card
- Insert the card
- Select the amount of money and press **enter**

2. Changing a wheel on a car
- Put the new wheel on and replace the wheel nuts
- Lower the car
- Place the jack under the car
- Tighten the wheel nuts
- Raise the car until the wheel is off the ground
- Loosen the wheel nuts
- Remove the wheel nuts and the wheel

3. Claiming expenses
- Fill in the claim form at the end of the month
- Give the form and the receipts to the accounts department
- Ask the head of your department to sign the form
- Keep your receipts

Giving instructions

First (of all)
Then/Next/After that   } insert...
At the same time
Finally

Don't forget to   } tighten...
Make sure you

A student is working with you for a week to get work experience. Think of a task and give some instructions on how to do it (e.g. using the fax machine).

ACTIVE AND PASSIVE

Active: We <u>serve</u> breakfast between 7 and 9 a.m.
           We <u>ask</u> guests to leave their rooms by 12:30 p.m.
Passive: Breakfast <u>is served</u> between 7 and 9 a.m.
           Guests <u>are asked</u> to leave their rooms by 12:30 p.m.

The passive is often used in written notices. The two passive sentences above come from a notice in a hotel room.

Look at these five active sentences.
● Say where they come from.
● Make them into passive sentences.

1. We ask visitors to sign the visitors' book.
2. We reserve this parking space for visitors.
3. We do not supply batteries with this unit.
4. We check every toy before it leaves the factory.
5. We only accept cheques with identification.

Now complete these sentences using the verbs below. Use **in** to say where the action happens or **by** to say who or what does it.

assemble   do   deliver   store   develop   print

e.g. All our books *are printed*   *in* Hong Kong.

6. New products _____ _____ the R and D department.
7. The tests _____ _____ a laboratory.
8. Most of our goods _____ _____ truck.
9. 70% of our cars _____ _____ robot.
10. The oil _____ _____ large tanks.

CHECK YOUR GRAMMAR: PAGE 92.

A MANUFACTURING PROCESS

Britt Elstrom is production manager at Norda Matches. Here she describes how matches are made. As you listen to her, choose a verb from the list for each step in the process (1–9 in the diagram).

cut   push   punch   add   clean   put into   coat   dry   transfer

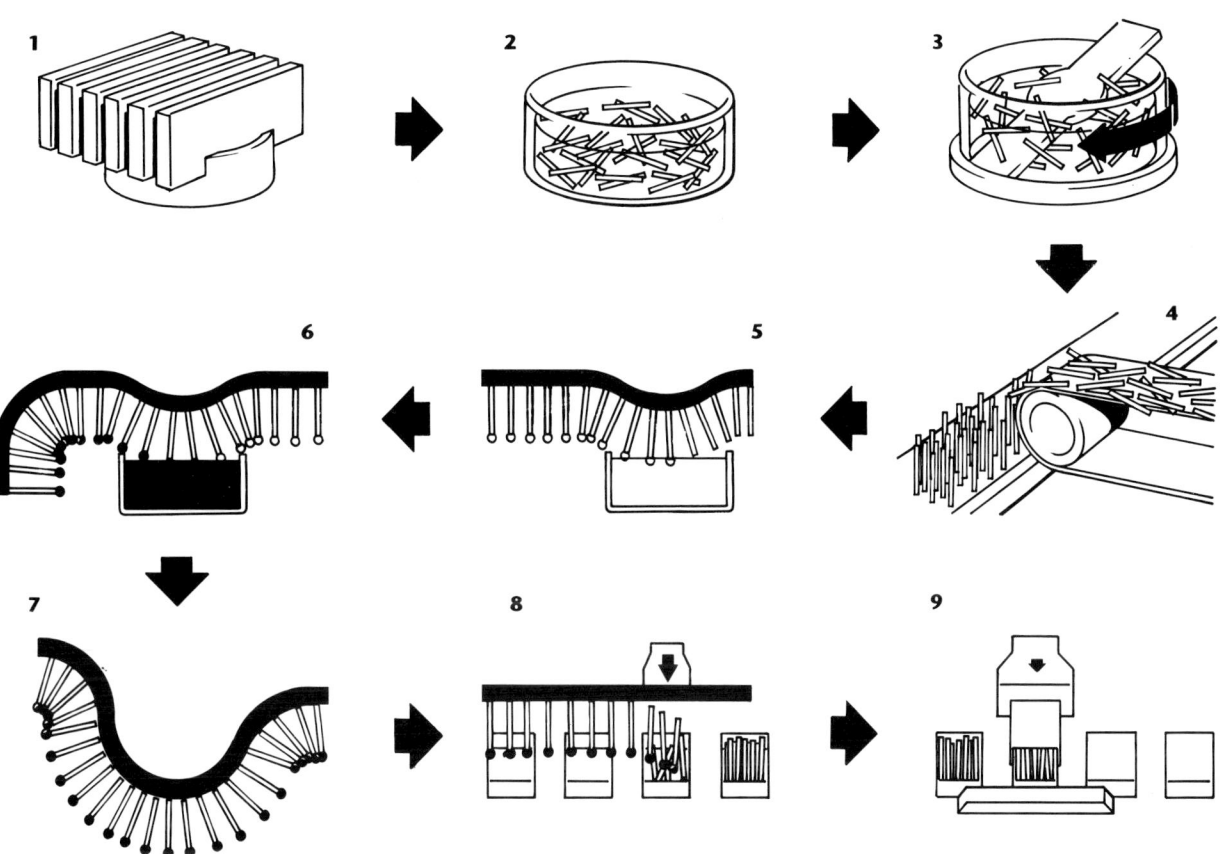

Now describe the process yourself. Begin like this: "First the logs are cut into thin sticks and then they are..."

11 A MANUFACTURING PROCESS

BRAINSTORMING

The new management of Norda Matches wants to improve efficiency. Choose one of the areas below and, using the language box to help you, say generally:

1. How quality can be controlled.
2. How internal communications can be improved.
3. How production costs can be reduced.
4. How administrative costs can be reduced.
5. How sales can be increased.
6. How staff can be motivated.

Describing methods

One way is to improve relations between...

In some companies bonuses are given.
In our company we have a weekly newsletter.

New technology can be introduced.
Regular tests can be done.

HOW THINGS ARE DONE

Prepare a short talk about a system or process that you know well. Choose from these areas:

1. Your country   e.g. the electoral system, the legal system, the educational system, etc.
2. Your company e.g. a production process, a decision-making process, employing and training new staff, etc.

Common Errors

The ~~robots~~ *cars* are assembled ~~the~~ ~~cars~~ *by robots*.

Children ~~are~~ start school at the age of five.

They are made ~~from~~ *by* Bader in Germany.

After key in your personal number. *(that)*

~~At last~~ *Finally* take your card out of the machine.

Read about KPS and say why it is successful.

The Kawasaki Production System

MORE and more Western manufacturers are taking an interest in KPS (Kawasaki Production System), a development of JIT (Just-in Time) manufacturing. JIT helps to reduce lead-time and work-in-progress. But JIT production uses smaller batch sizes and so machines have to be re-set often to produce different components. This requires more manpower and so JIT does not always increase productivity.

KPS can increase productivity because it adds flexibility to the process. The principle is simple: to continuously improve the production process to reduce waste - waste of manpower, time, and resources. These improvements are not achieved with expensive high-tech solutions, but with simple ideas. For example, in one Japanese factory, components are transferred from one machine to another by gravity – the beginning of the line is higher than the end.

The results of KPS speak for themselves. A Japanese crankshaft factory using KPS had 7 men operating 22 machines and producing 2700 pieces a week. The work-in-progress was 60 pieces. A similar U.K. factory had 37 men operating 25 machines and producing 1400 pieces a week. The work-in-progress was 6500 pieces. That is, 38 pieces per man per week in the U.K. and 386 pieces per man per week in Japan.

Vocabulary notes

lead-time	– the time a production process takes
work-in-progress	– products on the line or not finished
batch	– a quantity or group of the same products
waste	– using time, money, etc., badly
crankshaft	– part of an engine (which turns vertical or horizontal motion into circular motion)

SIZES, SHAPES AND MATERIALS

Study the words below and then try to think of things which have these qualities or features. Use a dictionary to help you.

Size	Shape	Material
large	square	plastic
small	round	glass
huge	circular	wood
tiny	oval	stone
long	rectangular	rubber
short	cylindrical	leather
thick	L-shaped	iron
thin	pointed	steel
3-metre		aluminium
50-mile		

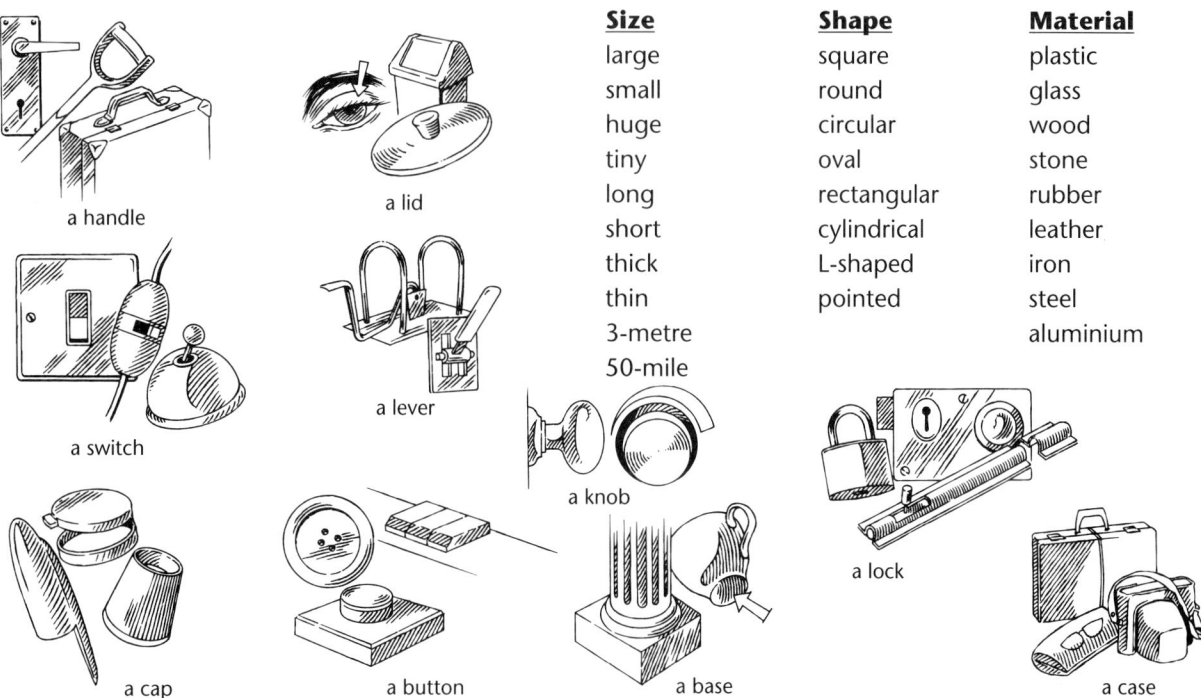

a handle
a lid
a switch
a lever
a knob
a lock
a cap
a button
a base
a case

12 A NEW PRODUCT

DESCRIBING PRODUCTS

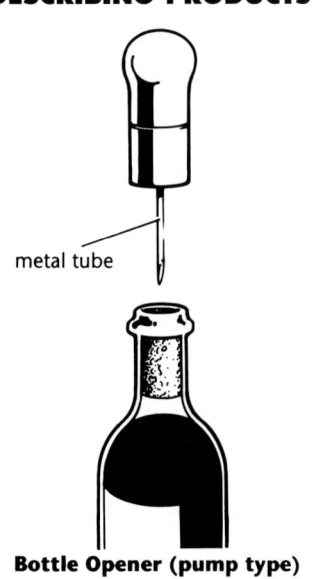

metal tube

Bottle Opener (pump type)

You work for a wholesale supplier of quality goods used in the home and office. Look at the pictures of four of these products and, using the language box to help you, describe one or two of them to a customer.

Describing things

It's a clothes brush.

It's used for cleaning...
It's for cleaning...

It's made of plastic and...

It consists of two parts.
It has a strong handle and...

It's easy to carry/use.
With this type of brush, you don't need to....

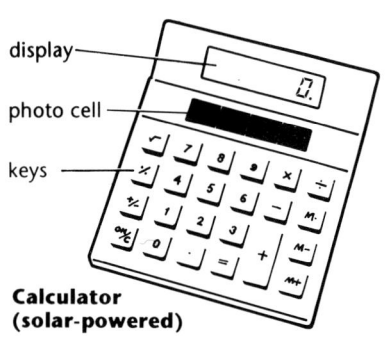

**Calculator
(solar-powered)**

display
photo cell
keys

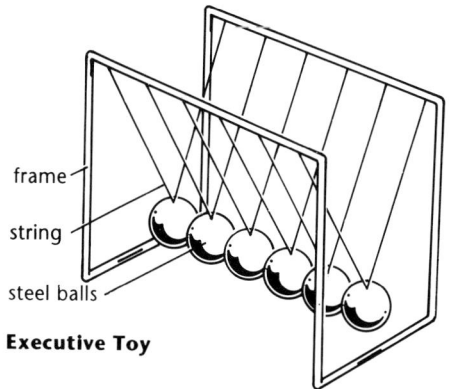

Executive Toy

frame
string
steel balls

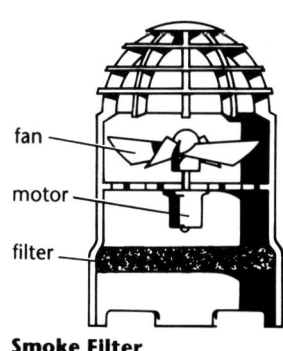

Smoke Filter

fan
motor
filter

Now choose one of the products and describe how it works. Look at the example first to help you.

e.g. It works a little like a bicycle pump. First you push the thin metal tube down through the cork. Then you pump air into the bottle. As the air is pumped into the bottle, the cork is pushed out.

THE BEST PRODUCT

Choose a word from the list to make a sentence about each product.

e.g. Duron makes the longest-lasting batteries on the market.
Lucis makes the most economical lightbulbs on the market.

| safe | accurate | powerful | comfortable |
| quiet | strong | economical | long-lasting |

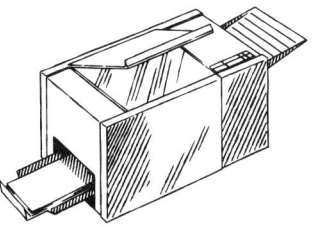

Zenon photocopiers

Matteson superglue

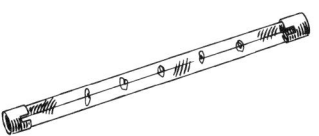

Lucis lightbulbs

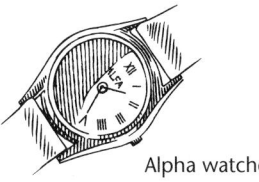

Alpha watches

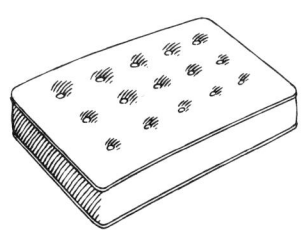

Comfit mattresses

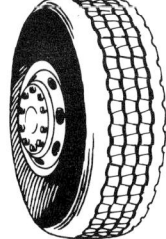

Firesteam tyres

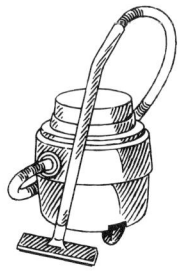

Evac vacuum cleaners

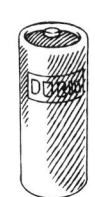

Duron batteries

CHECK YOUR GRAMMAR: PAGE 99.

PRODUCT FEATURES

Read the description of Philadelphia based company, B.J. Buckwald, and then complete the chart below.

B. J. BUCKWALD CUSTOM MOULDING INC.

Customer Support We supply plastic bottles and containers to the cosmetics and cleaning materials industries. Each one of our customers has different needs and those needs are changing all the time. So our aim is to be flexible. We offer products in a range of shapes, colors, and sizes (20 mm to 250 mm diameter) and we can make custom-built containers quickly and in any quantity (1000's to millions).

Service We also believe in rapid response: with a maximum of six weeks from order to delivery, we are the fastest and most flexible company in the North East.

R & D Our products are supplied with a range of different caps, including the latest designs. Design is an important part of our approach (18% of our budget goes on research and development).

Priorities And we are a company that cares about people and the environment. All our containers are made of 60% biodegradable material and many of our caps are designed to be childproof and safe.

Company Approach	**Product Features**
1. To be flexible.	1. A range of colours, shapes, and sizes.
2.	2.
3.	3.
4.	4.
	5.

A NEW PRODUCT

Two months ago, Carmen Keiller, a New York based cosmetics company, asked B.J. Buckwald to design a new bottle for their best-selling Jocasta shampoo.

Listen to the presentation of the new design given by B.J. Buckwald's account executive.

1. Decide which design he is describing, A, B or C.
2. Note down the reasons for this design.

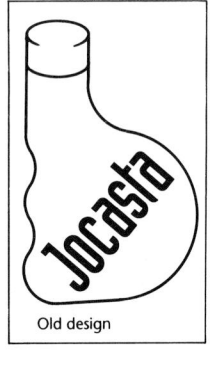

Old design

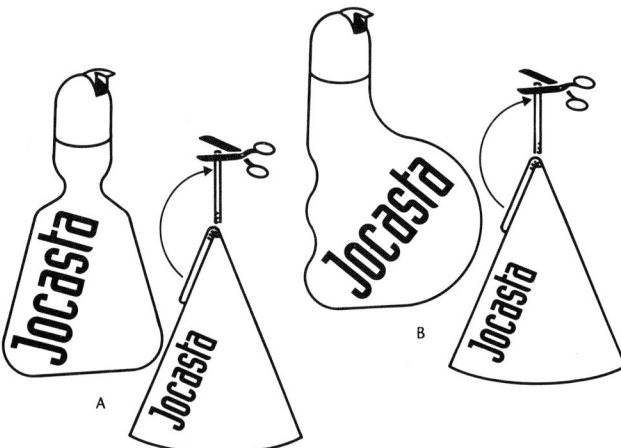

A

B

C

PRESENTING A PRODUCT

Now prepare a short presentation on a product you know well. Use the language box to help you.

Giving a presentation

I'd like to talk to you about...
I'm going to tell you about...

I'd like to divide my presentation into three parts.
First(ly)..., second(ly)..., and finally...

As you know...

So, what are the main features of...?
If we look at..., we can see that...
This means that...

Finally, I'd like to say that...
I think that's all. Now, if there are any questions...

Common Errors

It's the ~~safer~~ *safest* tyre on the market.
~~I tell~~ *I'd like to tell* you about...

AN ADVERTISING BRIEF Read the memo and the advertisement. Which features of the service did the advertising agency use in their advertisement?

LEAR & LEAR ADVERTISING

Memo   From: Charles Lear
                           To: James Selleck

Here are the brochures for Quartz Rent-a-Car. They want us to design an advertisement for them based on the following features:-

- Efficiency
- Competitive prices
- A large network (they are the second largest company in the market)
- Special rates for companies
- Unlimited mileage
- Many types of vehicle available

QUARTZ
Rent-a-Car
The Second Largest Car Rental Company in the World

Who was the second man on the moon?

What is the second tallest building in the world?

Which is the second largest computer company in the world?

No-one likes to be second best. That is why at Quartz we offer a service which is cheaper, more efficient, and more flexible than our main competitors. At Quartz we try harder to satisfy our customers, because we want to be the biggest **and** the best.

VERBS AND NOUNS Look at the list of nouns and then decide which of these five common verbs are possible with them.

make   take   do   give   have

*make, take*_____ a decision (about it)
_____ notes (on it)
_____ an appointment (with him)
_____ a deal (with her)
_____ research (into it)
_____ a profit/loss (on it)
_____ a suggestion
_____ a meeting/discussion (about it)
_____ a reason (for it)
_____ something (about it)

13 A FIVE-YEAR PLAN

EXPRESSING PURPOSE

Mitsuko Uno is personal assistant to the sales manager. Here are some of the things she did on her day off last week. Say why she did them. Look at the examples first.

e.g. She turned on the radio at 8 a.m. *to listen to the news*.
    She walked to the post office *to buy some stamps*.

1. She telephoned the travel agent _____.
2. She went to the market _____.
3. She stopped at the petrol ('gas' in U.S. English) station _____.
4. She went to the library _____.
5. She bought some glue _____.
6. She visited the museum _____.

PLANS AND INTENTIONS

Two weeks ago Satoru Ishiyama started a new job as production manager at Toida Automotive Products. He intends to make a number of changes in the department. Say why he is planning each change. Look at the example first.

e.g. He <u>is going to</u> introduce a bonus scheme <u>to</u> increase productivity (this is his decision).
    He <u>is thinking of</u> introduc<u>ing</u> a bonus scheme <u>to</u> increase productivity (this is his idea).

<u>**Intended Action**</u>	<u>**Purpose**</u>
introduce a bonus scheme	discuss production problems
visit the suppliers	improve efficiency
hold daily meetings with the production foreman	improve relations between workers and management
hold weekly meetings with union representatives	install new machinery
do a work study	increase productivity
close the factory for three days	negotiate new contracts

You are new in your department. First think of some changes you would like to make. Then say what you are going to do or are thinking of doing.

CHECK YOUR GRAMMAR: PAGE 86/106.

GOVERNMENT PLANS

Study the phrases and then find opposites from the list of verbs below.

build a new hospital	_____ an old hospital
encourage foreign investment	_____ foreign investment
privatize state industries	_____ large industries
set up a youth training programme	_____ a youth training programme
increase public spending	_____ public spending
appoint a new Minister for Transport	_____ the Minister for Transport

restrict	nationalize	reduce
dismiss/fire	close down	abolish

MAKING PREDICTIONS

There is going to be a national election. There are two main political parties, the Conservative (right-wing) Party and the Socialist (left-wing) Party. Say what each party will do about the following, if they win the election. First look at the example.

e.g. Employment: If the Conservatives win, they will (probably) set up a youth training programme (to create more jobs).

Taxes

Foreign trade

Military spending

Education

Industry

Transport

CHECK YOUR GRAMMAR: PAGE 86.

A FIVE-YEAR PLAN

Mr Harada is president of Toida Automotive Products (TAP). TAP has an annual turnover of $45 billion and is the seventh largest car producer in Japan. It has four divisions: Cars (with production plants in Osaka, Tokyo, and Nagoya), Car Components, Motorcycles, and Insurance Services.

You are going to hear Mr Harada speaking to TAP's shareholders about the future of the company. Before you listen to his speech, look at the information on the next page and predict what changes he will make to the company. Use the language box to help you.

Predicting

I (don't) think they will increase...

Perhaps they will reduce...
They will probably reduce...
I am sure they will reduce...

Percentage of total profits				
	Cars	**Car Components**	**Motorcycles**	**Insurance Services**
Last year	59%	21%	14%	6%
This year	46%	20%	18%	16%

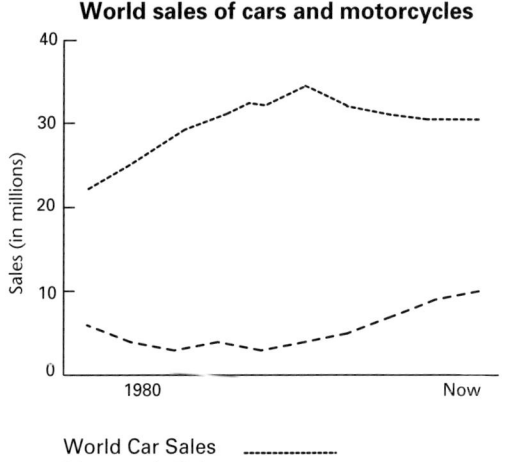

World sales of cars and motorcycles

World Car Sales ----------------
Motorcycle Sales - - - - - - -

Oil prices rise again

E.C. PUTS "GREEN TAX" ON CARS NO CHANGE FOR MOTORCYCLES

Mr Harada celebrates 80th birthday

Takeover possible as Northern Star Insurance share price rises

MASS PRODUCTION OF ELECTRIC CAR TO START IN U.S.

 Now listen and answer these questions.

1. What are Mr Harada's plans for the company?
2. What reasons does he give for the changes he is going to make?

Common Errors

He went to the bank ~~for getting~~ *to get* some money.

I ~~will~~ *am going to* buy a new car next week.

I will tell him, if I ~~will~~ see him.

I *don't* think the government will ~~not~~ increase taxes.

Study the profit and loss account and note where the difference between the budget and the total is more than 10,000. Give possible reasons for these differences.

e.g. Manufacturing costs were higher because the cost of supplies increased.

B&C Furniture
PROFIT AND LOSS ACCOUNT (YEAR TO DATE)

		YTD TOTAL		YTD BUDGET
Gross sales		3,107,219		3,049,200
Less discounts	(66,710)			
Less commission	(96,273)		(184,540)	
Net sales		2,944,236		2,864,660
Manufacturing costs	1,755,916		1,651,750	
Labour	433,423		403,590	
Delivery	108,685		103,460	
Less discounts received	(27,885)	2,270,139	(31,250)	2,127,550
Gross profit		674,097		737,110
Overheads				
Indirect selling costs	73,780		73,000	
Insurance	20,830		16,100	
Telephone/post	17,208		15,750	
Office	11,956		11,700	
Salaries	242,277		215,560	
Motor expenses	25,457		31,860	
Plant depreciation	9,257		9,800	
Legal and audit	7,182		6,150	
Heat/light/power	10,647		13,100	
Building maintenance	22,336		4,400	
Building depreciation	4,500		4,000	
Bad debts	15,000		18,000	
Finance costs-general	30,383		30,850	
Finance costs-loan	33,413		23,460	
Sundries	8,819		6,100	
Rent	20,250		20,000	
Management bonus	8,76			
New building costs	26,171	580,342		499,830
Net profit/loss A/C		93,755		237,280

FINANCE

Choose the best word from the list to complete each sentence.

turnover   capital   costs   forecast   budget   overheads

e.g. Our annual *turnover* is £35 million and 10% of this is profit.

1. The marketing department wants to increase its _____ by 15% next year.
2. We have a lot of _____ – heating, lighting, office supplies, rent, etc.
3. The _____ for next year is very good.
4. Salaries are 38% of our total _____.
5. We have a lot of _____ invested in these machines.

14

MAKING AN ARRANGEMENT

ARRANGING A MEETING

1. You want to arrange a meeting with Judy Whitlam to discuss her report. Telephone her and suggest lunch at the Carlton at one o'clock on Thursday.

2. You have an appointment with Mr Pardoe on Wednesday at 3 p.m., but you are very busy that day. Telephone him and change the appointment to another day.

Now study the dialogues below. Then listen and complete them.

Wayne	Hello, Judy. It's Wayne here. Look, I'd like to meet you to discuss your report.
Judy	O.K. Where _____ we meet?
Wayne	How _____ the Carlton? We _____ have lunch first.
Judy	That _____ great.
Wayne	Does Thursday _____ you?
Judy	Yes, that's _____. What time?
Wayne	I _____ meet you in the bar at one o'clock.
Judy	Good. See you then.

Janine	Hello, it's Janine here. I'm calling about our Wednesday appointment. I'm afraid I can't _____ it that day. Can we change it to another day?
Pardoe	Yes, that's O.K. When?
Janine	_____ about Thursday morning?
Pardoe	Thursday is fine.
Janine	Good. _____ we say 10:30?
Pardoe	10:30? 11:30 _____ me better.
Janine	O.K. I _____ see you on Thursday at 11:30.
Pardoe	Fine. Bye.

Now use the language box to help you make two more arrangements.

3. You want to show your PR officer, Brad Smith, around your company's new research centre. Invite him to come on Tuesday morning.

4. You want your marketing director, John Jones, to meet Sue Harding, your new agent in Jakarta. Suggest the Paris Cafe at 3 p.m. today.

Making arrangements

What/How about { my office?
{ meeting at my office?

We could meet at my office.

Where/What time shall we meet?
Shall we say 10 o'clock?
Does 10 o'clock suit you?

Great./Fine.
That sounds fine.

I'm sorry, I can't. I'm busy.
I can't make it on Wednesday.

I'll see you outside the cinema at 7 o'clock.

A VISIT FROM A VIP

Mr Dillinger, the president of your parent company, MM Holdings, is going to visit your company for two days next week to open a new research centre. You are in charge of his programme for the visit. Using the programme below, tell your boss what the arrangements are. Begin like this: "He is arriving at the airport at 3 p.m. on Tuesday. JB is meeting him there. Then he is having..."

ITINERARY FOR VISIT OF **MR DILLINGER** – PRESIDENT MM HOLDINGS

Tuesday	3:00	Arrives at airport (JB to meet him)	**Wednesday**	9:00	Meeting with FW
	4:00	Meeting and drinks with MM management		10:00	Opens new research centre
				11:00	Press conference
	5:30	Hotel		1:00	Lunch with local VIP's
	8:00	Sydney Opera House with FW		2:30	Boat trip around Sydney Harbour
				7:40	Plane leaves

Copies to Frank Warren (Managing Director) and Julian Barnes (Personnel Manager)

CHECK YOUR GRAMMAR: PAGE 87.

MAKING AN ARRANGEMENT

STUDENT A

You are Norman Barry, an old friend of Mr Dillinger. Telephone him at his hotel and arrange to see him before he leaves. You are free all evening on Tuesday and on Wednesday between 12 and 2 and after 4:30.

STUDENT B

You are Mr Dillinger. You receive a call from your old friend Norman Barry. Check your programme before you make any arrangements.

LISTEN AND SPEAK

You are going to show Mr Dillinger around the new research centre. Listen to what he says and reply in a natural way.

● Mr Dillinger's arrival
● At the research centre

15   A PROGRESS REPORT

HISTORICAL EVENTS

Complete each sentence with a verb and a date from the list.

unify	build	found	launch	open	sign	invent	write
1926	1906	1990	210BC	1597	1914	1957	1957

e.g. The Treaty of Rome *was* *signed* in *1957*.

1. The Panama Canal _____ _____ in _____.
2. Romeo and Juliet _____ _____ in _____.
3. The first communications satellite _____ _____ in _____.
4. The Great Wall of China _____ _____ in _____.
5. Rolls Royce _____ _____ in _____.
6. East and West Germany _____ _____ in _____.
7. Television _____ _____ in _____.

CHECK YOUR GRAMMAR: PAGE 92.

COMPANY HISTORY

Here are some notes on important events in the history of Banque Metropole (Metropolitan Bank). Add the dates given below and describe the company's history. Begin like this: "Metropolitan Bank was founded over 80 years ago in Dijon by Georges Marquet. It expanded rapidly during the 1920s and branches..."

- founded by Georges Marquet
- expands rapidly: branches opened in Paris, Marseilles, and Lyon
- Marquet killed in a plane crash
- taken over by Marquet's two sons, Pierre and Hubert
- merges with Banque Liègeois de Commerce (BLC)
- international branches opened in London, Milan, Geneva, and Frankfurt
- directors of BLC fired in a scandal
- Christophe Marquet appointed president

during the 1920's	after the war	the following year	
in July 1980	over 80 years ago	in 1936	last year

Now describe some important events in your company's (or country's) history. First make notes to help you.

AN UPDATE

Christophe Marquet is having dinner with Margit Schultz, head of the international marketing department at Metropolitan Bank. They are discussing a campaign to promote the bank's free advice service for customers.

Listen to the tape and answer the questions.

What have they done about...
1. information leaflets?
2. advertising?
3. advice for small businesses?

What does she say about...
4. the results?
5. the cost?

CHECK YOUR GRAMMAR: PAGE 89.

SURVEY RESULTS

Metropolitan Bank talked to 200 of its employees to find out about levels of stress. Look at the information below and use the language box to help you describe the results of the survey.

Question	Response	
	Yes	No
Do you smoke?	64	136
Do you travel to work by car?	162	38
Do you sleep more than 8 hours?	0	200
Do you own a house?	93	107
Do you have any children?	88	112
Do you live in the city?	187	13
Do you work over 40 hours a week?	21	179
Do you take work home with you?	14	186
Do you play any sports?	48	152

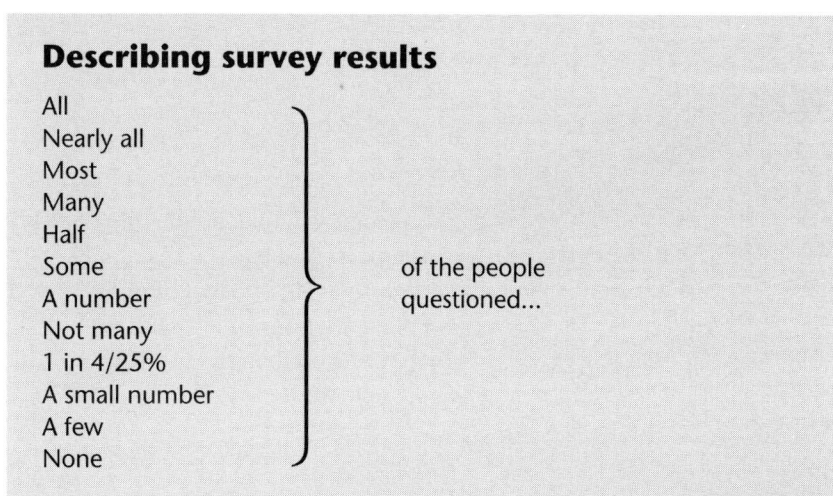

Describing survey results

All
Nearly all
Most
Many
Half
Some   of the people
A number   questioned...
Not many
1 in 4/25%
A small number
A few
None

15 A PROGRESS REPORT

A PROGRESS REPORT

You work for the National Development Bank (NDB). The NDB gives loans for projects which will help local communities and local businesses. There are progress reports on two of these projects below. Study one of them and, as you read, complete the fact sheet on the next page. Then ask someone for the information you need to complete the other fact sheet.

STUDENT A

The Beazely Housing Project was launched by the Beazely Housing Association (BHA) three years ago with a National Development Bank loan of £64 million. The aim of the project is to provide the people of the Beazely area with better housing and better local facilities.

The BHA have built 150 houses, half the proposed number, and have completed an expensive road building programme. All of the new houses are now occupied, but many of them by people from outside the Beazely area. Some local residents have said that the new houses are too expensive for them. They are unhappy because the BHA has spent a lot of the money on roads and not enough on cheap housing. In fact, they have already spent over the original £64 million.

A number of new businesses have moved to the area and the BHA now wants other companies to come to Beazely. It has asked the bank for a second loan of £28 million to complete the building programme and build a business park. In their new proposal, they have reduced the total number of houses to 200.

STUDENT B

The Anglia Fruit Co-operative (AFC) was founded two years ago to help small fruit farms in the South East of Britain to compete with the larger British and European fruit producers. The National Development Bank financed the project with a loan of £8.4 million. The AFC has already spent £7 million of this loan and will begin repayments this year.

The results of the project have been excellent. The AFC has used the money to build a packing plant and two new warehouses and it has invested in transport to distribute the goods. Production in the area has also increased but not all farmers have joined the co-operative.

The AFC has negotiated agreements with two major British supermarket chains and is now looking for other deals. One problem is that the products are not well-known outside Britain and exports have not increased. The AFC now needs more money (£6m) to market their products in Europe but it is difficult to say how big this market is.

```
Project: ............................................................
Date started: ..............................................
Aims:.............................................................
Action taken: ...............................................

................................................................
Money spent: ...............................................
Positive results:...........................................
Negative results:..........................................
Future plans: ...............................................
Money needed:.............................................
```

```
Project: ............................................................
Date started: ..............................................
Aims:.............................................................
Action taken: ...............................................

................................................................
Money spent: ...............................................
Positive results:...........................................
Negative results:..........................................
Future plans: ...............................................
Money needed:.............................................
```

Using the information you now have, decide if you want to lend the extra money for each project.

Common Errors

written
It was ~~write~~ by Shakespeare.

She ~~has~~ left three years ago.

Have they had
~~Had they~~ good results this year?

the
All of ∧ employees have four weeks holiday.

Read the report and guess what these words mean.

complaint   victim   compensation   refund   withdraw

CONFIDENTIAL

INTERNAL REPORT

We have received a number of complaints about our "Contour" car seats and we have decided to stop production while tests are done. We have also asked retailers to return their stocks of these seats to us.

As you know, the "Contour" seat is designed to mould itself to the shape of the driver's body. However, some people have said that in hot weather they cannot get out of the seat easily. One man actually had to leave his trousers in his car and walk to a telephone to get help. Other drivers have said they were in pain after driving in the seat for a long time.

So far, we have not had to pay compensation, but we have refunded money to over 100 dissatisfied customers. There have not been any reports in the newspapers yet but if there are, we will probably have to withdraw the seat from the market completely.

Check your guesses with a dictionary.

PERSONAL CHARACTERISTICS

What qualities do these people need for their work? Choose from the list below.

persuasive	calm	hard-working
creative	honest	open-minded
decisive	tough	understanding
cautious	thorough	sociable
ambitious	patient	reliable

Salesman	General Manager	Development Engineer	Personnel Manager

/ə/ as in i**sn**'t   /ɪzənt/

/ə/ is a very common sound in English. Syllables which are not stressed often have this sound. Listen to these words and practise saying them.

persuasive   patient   open-minded
thorough   ambitious   understanding
reliable   sociable   cautious

16   A PERSONNEL PROBLEM

SHOULD AND SHOULDN'T   Look at the sentences below and, using the verbs given, say what is the right, or wrong, thing to do in each situation.

e.g. She is the right person for the job. (give)

We <u>should give</u> her the job.

1. They have made a good offer. (accept)
2. She is unhappy in her department. (transfer)
3. His advice is bad advice. (take)
4. Only two people have applied for the training course next week. (cancel)
5. There is a lot to discuss with them. (arrange)
6. Smoking in the plant is dangerous. (allow)
7. There are several possible solutions. (choose)

CHECK YOUR GRAMMAR: PAGE 95.

GIVING OPINIONS   Mark (X) the subjects you want to talk about on the next page. Then ask other people for their opinions. Use the language box to help you with the discussion.

> ## Giving opinions
>
> What do you feel about military service?
> Do you think that people should do military service?
>
> I (don't) think military service is a good idea.
> In my opinion, military service is a bad thing.
>
> I (don't) agree with it/you.
> I disagree with you/military service.
> That's (not) true.
>
> Yes, but...
> That's not the point.
>
> In general.../On the whole...
>
> In France, for example, military service is...
> In places like/such as France, military service is...
>
> It depends on the person/the country/the time etc.
> It depends on how you look at it.

1. Dangerous sports like boxing should not be allowed.
2. There should be more women doing important jobs.
3. Everyone should do military service.
4. You should never smack your children.
5. People should have the freedom to say or write what they like.
6. Strikes are usually due to bad management.
7. The aim of education is to prepare children for work.

Listen to the tape.
- Which subject is each person talking about?
- What is his/her opinion about it?

Subject	Opinion
Education	Disagrees. He thinks we should teach independence.

PERSONNEL MANAGEMENT

Here are some of the functions of a personnel manager. Look at the notice board and match each notice with a function from the list.

- to give advice on pensions
- to help with personal problems
- to encourage health and safety
- to recruit new staff
- to discuss salaries
- to train staff

A **ONE-WEEK COURSE IN TIME MANAGEMENT**
Apply Christchurch Avenue
Tel: 02356 890123

B **Unhappy at Work or at Home ?**
See Angela Madison

C **WANTED** Machine Tool Operators

D **New Overtime Rates of Pay**
Grade 1   46
Grade 2   27
Grade 3   18
Grade 4   16

E **Worried About Retirement?**

F **ALWAYS WEAR PROTECTIVE GOGGLES IN THE PLANT**

G **Give up Smoking NOW**

A PERSONNEL PROBLEM

You are in charge of your company's personnel abroad. You are visiting the office in Mexico City. Elvira Ramirez, general manager in Mexico, has some staff problems there. What should she do about them?

1. The new head of sales, Nigel Thomson, wants his family to join him in Mexico, but this is not part of his contract. If they cannot join him, he says he will have to leave the job and go back to them.
2. Joaquim Vacares has worked in the Mexico office since it opened 20 years ago. He says he is going to retire at the end of this year.
3. The office has a new computer system, but so far only two people have learned how to use it. There is no time during working hours to learn the new system and no-one wants to stay after work.
4. Two months ago you wrote a letter to Elvira telling her to reduce staff costs by 20%. She is worried that there will be a strike, if she tries to reduce the workforce by so much.

A PUZZLE

Try to find the best solution to this problem.

Two companies merge, but the presidents of each company, Mr Sly and Mr Smart, cannot decide who will be president of the new company. They are standing in the car park when Mr Sly says, "I know what we can do. I will put two stones, one white and one black, into a bag. Then you choose one of them. If it's black, I will be president and if it's white, you will be president." Mr Smart agrees, but he sees Mr Sly put two black stones into the bag.

What should Mr Smart do if he wants the job?

Common Errors

We should ~~to~~ tell him.

I ~~am~~ agree with you.

should
You ~~have to~~ take an aspirin.

It depends
~~It's depend~~ on you.

M
~~The~~ ~~m~~ilitary service is a good idea.

Study the training plan and then use it to make a training programme for staff in one department of your company.

TRAINING PLAN

General Plan   **Example**

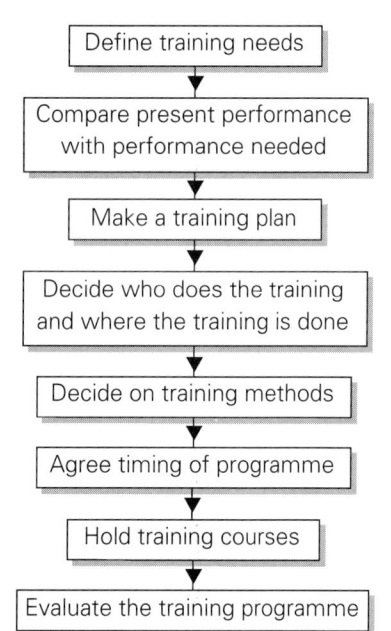

Define training needs

General managers need to be able to deal with personnel problems.

Compare present performance with performance needed

At the moment they usually ask the personnel department to deal with problems.

Make a training plan

A five-day course.

Decide who does the training and where the training is done

An outside consultant will run the course at the company training centre.

Decide on training methods

Lectures, seminars, and role play.

Agree timing of programme

Early September.

Hold training courses

Ask participants to bring examples of specific problems with them.

Evaluate the training programme

Have staff relations improved?

IDIOMS

Look at the dialogues and study the underlined idioms. Think how to say the same thing in your language. Check in a dictionary to see if you are right.

A <u>What's the matter</u>?
B The machine has <u>broken down</u>.
A Not again! We should <u>get rid of</u> it.

A When shall we meet?
B <u>It's up to you</u>.
A How about Thursday?...No, Friday...no, Monday.
B Well, <u>make up your mind</u>.

A <u>Hurry up</u>! We're late.
B <u>Come off it</u>! It's only 6:30.

A <u>Is something wrong with</u> your car?
B Well, I've <u>run out of</u> petrol ('gas' in U.S. English).
A Can I <u>give you a lift</u> to the petrol ('gas') station?
B Thanks. That's very kind of you.

17 A JOINT VENTURE

DISCUSSING OPTIONS

Listen to the tape.
● What is each conversation about?
● What options are open to the speakers?

Now complete these sentences using one of these two forms:
If + present simple _____, _____ **will** _____.
If + past simple _____, _____ **would** _____.

e.g. If you _look_ (look) at the results of the market research, you _will_ _see_ (see) that people want a drink that is healthy.

1. If more people _____ (think) Rico was a healthy product, its sales _____ _____ (increase).
2. But if the company _____ (change) the packaging, _____ it really _____ (help) Rico's image?
3. Perhaps they _____ only _____ (change) the image, if they _____ (give) Rico a new name.
4. If they _____ (stay) where they are now, they _____ (have) to expand and modernize their factory.
5. The Düsseldorf site _____ _____ (be) a better option, if it _____ (be) nearer to the company's main suppliers.
6. There is a danger that if they _____ (move) to Düsseldorf, they _____ _____ (lose) many of their skilled workers.

CHECK YOUR GRAMMAR: PAGE 90.

MINI NEGOTIATIONS

Study these situations and decide:
● which role to take.
● your negotiating position.
Then act out the situations, using the language box to help you.

1. Participants: **Employer and employee**
     Situation: Employer wants to send employee to the Paris office for two years. Employee wants to go, but for a minimum of three years.

     Negotiate: Salary (at present £24,000, but Paris is more expensive)
                 Help with moving costs
                 Number of years

2. Participants:	Union representative and management representative
Situation:	Union wants a reduction in the number of working hours per week from 40 to 38. Management will consider this but only on certain conditions.
Negotiate:	Increase in productivity (productivity 60% at present) Basic salary Special orders (where time is important for contracts)

Negotiating

Opening	Let me outline our position. Our position is this...
Making proposals	If you could guarantee/promise us..., we would/could... If you did X, we would/could do Y. Would you be able to...? In return, we would/could... We could offer you a discount of, say, 25%.
Rejecting Accepting	That would be difficult for us. That sounds fine.
Buying time	Perhaps we can come back to that point later. I would need to discuss that with my... I'll have to think about that.
Summarizing	Fine, so can we agree that...?

THE HI-FI MARKET

Read the text and answer the questions.
1. What are the two types of market for hi-fi equipment?
2. What do the consumers in each market buy?

This Month's Best Buys ...

Omnisonic
Midi System OM800

This compact midi system is good quality and good value for money. It is a complete system consisting of dual tape deck, FM tuner, CD player, amplifier (output: 25 watts per channel) with built-in graphic equalizer and 3-way loudspeakers. The unit comes in a smart grey aluminium case. With digital display and easy to use controls, it will appeal to the average user.

* * * * *

For the specialist we have put together an attractive package of individual units which use the latest technology in digital recording. Beta Digital say that the BD10 is probably the best CD player on the market. We are not going to disagree with this, but at $4000 it is also one of the most expensive. To accompany it, we have chosen: the Leon D2A digital-analogue converter, the Sendor 200S, a 200-watt digital amplifier with remote control, and finally, Q4 speakers. The speakers use a 20 cm bass driver, 10 cm mid-range cone, and 2 cm tweeter to give a high quality sound. And the total price? At over $15,000 we recommend you see your bank manager first!

A JOINT VENTURE

Beta Digital is a young British company which produces specialist hi-fi equipment. At the moment it manufactures only CD players, but it is planning to expand its range. It markets the CD players in Britain and also, from an office in Los Angeles, to a few outlets in the Unites States.

XL Audio is a dealer, also based in Britain, which sells hi-tech audio equipment – speakers, amplifiers, etc. – from several leading European manufacturers.

Last week Al Feinstock, Beta Digital's representative in L.A., received a letter from Gary Levin, XL Audio's sales manager. In it Levin proposed a deal: that Beta Digital and XL Audio could market their products together in the U.S. Feinstock wrote back that he liked the idea very much and arranged a meeting at the L.A. office to hear more about it.

Look at your brief and prepare some notes before your meeting.

STUDENT A

You are Al Feinstock.

You can offer:
- To sell XL Audio's products in the U.S. through your existing outlets.
- A two-year contract (until your company has more of its own products on the market).

You want:
- 16% commission on XL Audio sales.
- All dealings with U.S. clients to be handled by you.
- Technical back-up for repairs and after-sales service.
- The right to sell goods from some of XL Audio's competitors.

STUDENT B

You are Gary Levin.

You can offer:
- To supply goods to go with Beta's CD players (amplifiers, speakers, etc.).
- 10–12% commission on sales of your products.
- Visits by one of XL Audio's engineers four times a year for servicing and repairs.

You want:
- A three-year contract.
- An introduction to Beta's U.S. contacts at the end of three years.
- An exclusive agency agreement.

During the negotiation try to reach an agreement because it is in both your interests to do so.

Common Errors

```
          had
If I would have more time, I would...
    will
I help, if I can.
  ^
      would
What will you do in my position?

A three-years contract.
```

Read the agency agreement and answer the questions.

An agreement was made this 21st June 1991 between Kurt Rauh A.G., hereinafter called the Principal, and Casa Blanca S.A., hereinafter called the Agent.

IT IS AGREED THAT:

1. The Principal appoints the Agent to be his sole representative.
2. The agency shall begin on this day and continue until 20th June 1993.
3. The Agent shall try at all times to promote the sales of the Principal's goods and will not sell products of a similar type for any other person or company.
4. The Principal shall pay a commission of 12% of the f.o.b. price on sales in the Agent's territory.
5. All orders received by the Agent shall be transmitted to the Principal.
6. The Principal reserves the right to refuse any such order.
7. The Agent shall not offer the credit of the Principal without the written permission of the Principal.

Signed this day of 21st June 1991.

The Principal
Kurt Rauh A.G.

K. Popper

K. POPPER

The Agent
Casa Blanca S.A.

J. Cortez

J. CORTEZ

Are these sentences true or false?

1. The contract is for three years.
2. Casa Blanca is the only agent for Kurt Rauh in Mexico.
3. Casa Blanca cannot pass orders to other companies.
4. Casa Blanca can never offer credit to its customers.

PHRASAL VERBS

Study these sentences and then use the underlined verbs to make your own sentences.

1. Could you <u>look after</u> our guests tomorrow? I am going to be away.
2. Excuse me. I'm <u>looking for</u> Mrs Carter's office. Is this the right floor?
3. I'm really <u>looking forward</u> to my holiday. I haven't had one for over a year.
4. You should <u>look at</u> this report. It's very interesting.

Look is just one of many verbs which has a special meaning when it is used with certain prepositions. Look at these other phrasal verbs and then make your own sentences with them.

5. Talestone Publishing wants to expand: it is trying to <u>take over</u> the Daily Sketch newspaper.
6. We have decided to <u>set up</u> an office in Brazil because we think it will be an important market in the future.
7. We are going to <u>put off</u> our decision until next week when we will have more information.
8. This is just the prototype. We need to <u>carry out</u> more tests before we are ready to go into production.
9. Ergat is going to close down its plant in York and <u>lay off</u> 600 workers.

18 TAKING PART IN A MEETING

PRESENTING AN ARGUMENT

Caldrone is a small Italian company, based in Turin, which makes ovens. Recently they have had problems with the clock-timers on their ovens. These clock-timers are supplied by Fantoni Inc. and Caldrone's managers are having a meeting to decide if they should look for a new supplier. Read what the purchasing manager says at the meeting and use the phrases to complete his argument.

the point is   on the other hand   anyway   that is to say   for example

Purchasing Manager	It will not be easy to find the right supplier, _____ a company which can supply good quality clocks at a good price. Fantoni's designs are not very modern, but _____ their clocks are cheap and reliable.
Sales Manager	What do you mean? Last month we had to send fifty back.
Purchasing Manager	_____ we know them and they know us. If we use another company, Sikur, _____, we have to start from the beginning again and _____ Fantoni is trying to improve reliability.

TAKING PART IN A MEETING

Caldrone decides to look for a new supplier of clock-timers for their ovens. Caldrone makes two types of oven in the medium price range, the Maestro, and the slightly more expensive Contessa. In the past, they have used different clock-timers for each type of oven, but it is possible to use the same one.

Use the information chart on the next page to choose a new supplier or suppliers. Then prepare to take part in a meeting. In the meeting, establish your criteria before you discuss the different suppliers.

Running a meeting

Starting

O.K. Shall we begin?

As you know,...

The aim/purpose of this meeting is to...
We are here to...

Can we begin by deciding/summarizing...?

Concluding

So, can we all agree that...?

O.K. I think that's all.
Well, we should stop there.

	Name of supplier (clock-timer)	Nearest distributor (in km)	Quality and features (1)	Reliability (2)	Order processing (3)	Quoted price ($ per 100)	Comments
Old Supplier	FANTONI (Super)	Trieste (540 km)	C	*	3 days	1000	
	JOHNSON (U.K.) (Imp)	Southampton (1100 km)	C	****	1-2 weeks	1000	They are very open to ideas and suggestions about design, new features, etc.
	CYCLOX (Italy) (Mark III)	Turin (3 km).	C	**	48 hours	900	Good after-sales service
	SIKUR (Switzerland) (Suretime)	Zurich (300 km)	A	*****	48 hours	1800	Has an excellent reputation and offers a 5-year guarantee on all clock-timers.
	FINSTIM (Switzerland) (Precision)	Frauenfeld (340 km)	B	****	2-3 days	1400	Supplies many leading manufacturers of domestic appliances.
	CHRONOME (France) (900)	Grenoble (180 km)	D	**	36 hours	700	Supplies Caldrone's main Italian competitor.
	PANAKRON (Japan) (Minutemaster)	Milan (160 km)	A	****	24 hours	1500	Has a good reputation for being efficient and easy to deal with.
	RELIANTE (Italy) (Certo)	Bologna (370 km)	B	***	3 days	1100	These clocks have very unusual designs.
	ESTHER (Spain) (Ahora)	Barcelona (780 km)	C	****	4-6 days	1000	A history of strikes, but it is now under new management.

(1) quality of materials used and the number of features on each clock-timer on a scale from A to E (A = excellent)
(2) based on statistical research (***** = very reliable; * = unreliable)
(3) time taken from receiving an order to delivery of the goods

CORRESPONDENCE

REASONS FOR WRITING

Letters in English often begin with the reason for writing. Look at the opening words of seven different letters and complete the sentences, using the phrases on the right.

e.g. I am writing to confirm our meeting next Tuesday.

I am writing to confirm...	...your letter of 25 June.
I am writing to apologize...	...for the delay.
I am writing in answer to...	...our meeting next Tuesday.
I am writing to thank you...	...about your English courses.
I am writing to inquire...	...the order we received.
I am writing to inform you...	...for sending me the books.
I am writing regarding...	...that I will not be able to come to your reception.

TYPES OF LETTER

Study the four letters below and on the next page and say what kind of letter each is.

1.

Colehouse Associates
20 EYOT PLACE, BATH BA1 4XT

Kerstin Security Systems
Kerstin House
High Street
Oxford OX1 7QP   18th September, 1991

Dear Sirs,

We are writing concerning the security locks (B 701) described on page 23 of your catalogue, which we received yesterday.

It is not clear if the locks can be used on all types of windows or are only suitable for use with wooden windows. Please could you advise us on this. We enclose specifications of the windows we intend to fit the locks to.

We look forward to hearing from you.

Yous faithfully,

Charlotte Rubah

CHARLOTTE RUBAH

An inquiry (checking facts or requesting information)
A covering letter (explaining something)
A thank-you letter
An invitation

2.

KERSTIN SECURITY SYSTEMS

KERSTIN HOUSE HIGH ST. OXFORD OX1 7QP

Mr V Hannah
Gees Hardware Store
Godstone Road
Banbury   OX3 9JG

6 June 1991

Dear Mr Hannah,

Thank you for your inquiry about our smoke alarms.

Please find enclosed a brochure and a copy of our price list for this year. You will see that we are offering a special discount on our Little Gem range until the end of next month.

Please contact us if you require any further information.

Yours sincerely,

Thomas O'Gorman

Thomas O'Gorman
(Sales Dept.)

3.

INSTITUTE OF MEDICINES & PHARMACEUTICAL PREPARATIONS

FERN HOUSE, BRIDGEWATER ROAD, EXETER, DEVON. EX9 2AP

G K Winkel
Marketing Manager
Reach Pharmaceuticals
31004 Zurich
Switzerland

September 23rd 1992

Dear Mr Winkel,

I do not know if you remember me - we met at the Healthcare Exhibition in Zurich last year.

We are holding another conference on *Pharmaceuticals and the Law* in Paris from March 12-16 and we would be very pleased if you could participate. Perhaps you would also like to speak to the conference about the law in Switzerland?

I look forward to hearing from you and hope very much that you will be able to attend.

Yours sincerely,

Brian Corbin

Brian Corbin

4.

Heelmann Winters Consultants

Sarah Warton
Communications Officer
CODATA plc
1-3 Prideaux Place
Southampton SO6 7DY

4th February 1991

Dear Sarah,

I am writing to thank you for your help and advice with my research. I am sorry that I have not written before, but I have been very busy.

It was very kind of you to meet me last week and discuss my paper on Customer Training - your suggestions and comments were very useful. I will, of course, send you a copy of the full report as soon as it is ready.

Please contact me the next time you come to Holland. I would be delighted to meet you again. Give my regards to your colleagues in the Communications Department.

Yours,

Piet Winters

Piet Winters

COMMON EXPRESSIONS

Decide what these phrases mean and put them into three groups.

please find enclosed   with regard to   regarding   best wishes to   attached is

concerning   **give my regards to**   **we enclose**

please find enclosed

CORRESPONDENCE

You are going to write one letter and reply to another.
Read your instructions and use the correspondence above to help you.

STUDENT A	**STUDENT B**
Write a letter:	**Write a letter:**
You receive this fax from the Grand Hotel. You wanted a single room, 3–5 June. Write and check the details.	You want to make a promotional video about your company. Write and invite Mr Sherman, a film-maker, to discuss this with you over lunch.

STUDENT A:

> Confirmation of booking: Regency Suite, 3–5 May at $258 a night.

STUDENT A — Reply to a letter:
Read the invitation from Student B and write back saying you cannot help him at the moment because you have a lot of other work.

STUDENT B — Reply to a letter:
Read the inquiry from Student A and write back giving the correct information (below) and apologizing for the mistake.

> Confirmation of booking: Single Room, 3–5 June, at $85 a night.

20 REVIEW

SURVIVAL ENGLISH

You are in London on business. Start at square 1 and follow a route to the bottom of the chart. In each situation, say what seems most natural and choose a reply to continue.

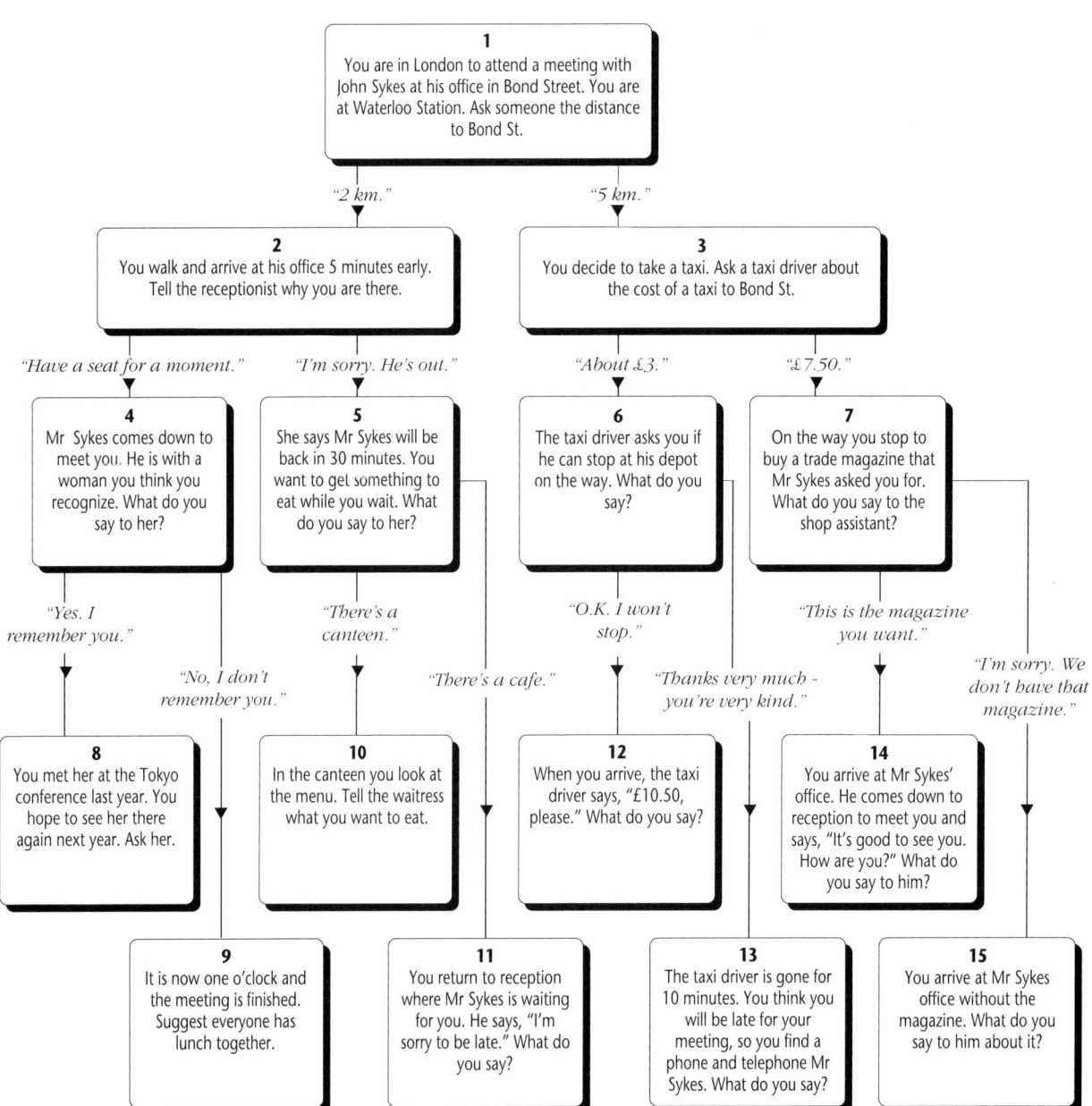

1
You are in London to attend a meeting with John Sykes at his office in Bond Street. You are at Waterloo Station. Ask someone the distance to Bond St.

"2 km."

"5 km."

2
You walk and arrive at his office 5 minutes early. Tell the receptionist why you are there.

3
You decide to take a taxi. Ask a taxi driver about the cost of a taxi to Bond St.

"Have a seat for a moment."

"I'm sorry. He's out."

"About £3."

"£7.50."

4
Mr Sykes comes down to meet you. He is with a woman you think you recognize. What do you say to her?

5
She says Mr Sykes will be back in 30 minutes. You want to get something to eat while you wait. What do you say to her?

6
The taxi driver asks you if he can stop at his depot on the way. What do you say?

7
On the way you stop to buy a trade magazine that Mr Sykes asked you for. What do you say to the shop assistant?

"Yes. I remember you."

"There's a canteen."

"O.K. I won't stop."

"This is the magazine you want."

"No, I don't remember you."

"There's a cafe."

"Thanks very much - you're very kind."

"I'm sorry. We don't have that magazine."

8
You met her at the Tokyo conference last year. You hope to see her there again next year. Ask her.

10
In the canteen you look at the menu. Tell the waitress what you want to eat.

12
When you arrive, the taxi driver says, "£10.50, please." What do you say?

14
You arrive at Mr Sykes' office. He comes down to reception to meet you and says, "It's good to see you. How are you?" What do you say to him?

9
It is now one o'clock and the meeting is finished. Suggest everyone has lunch together.

11
You return to reception where Mr Sykes is waiting for you. He says, "I'm sorry to be late." What do you say?

13
The taxi driver is gone for 10 minutes. You think you will be late for your meeting, so you find a phone and telephone Mr Sykes. What do you say?

15
You arrive at Mr Sykes office without the magazine. What do you say to him about it?

VOCABULARY REVIEW

1. Find the opposites.

to arrange	*to cancel*	expensive	*cheap*
to agree	_____	thick	_____
to remember	_____	fast	_____
to rise	_____	safe	_____
to win	_____	huge	_____
to sell	_____	right	_____

2. Complete the pairs.

stocks and	*shares*	import and	_____
research and	_____	health and	_____
supply and	_____	profit and	_____

3. Give another...

...method of payment	cheque,	*cash, credit card*
...person who buys	customer,	_____
...place where things are manufactured	factory,	_____
...document which gives information about products	catalogue,	_____
...word for a cut in price	reduction,	_____
...type of metal	iron,	_____
...thing companies sell	products,	_____
...document asking for payment	bill,	_____

4. Group the words into six families.

meetings	production	marketing	finance	communications	personnel
discuss	*machine*	*promotion*	*budget*	*letter*	*pension*
_____	_____	_____	_____	_____	_____
_____	_____	_____	_____	_____	_____
_____	_____	_____	_____	_____	_____
_____	_____	_____	_____	_____	_____
_____	_____	_____	_____	_____	_____

component	staff	overheads	comment	fax
memo	brand	lay off	operate	lever
advertisement	assemble	image	retire	chairperson
recruit	profit	recommend	report	costs
agenda	turnover	launch	process	campaign
attend	inquiry	message	loss	training

Pronunciation Practice

In this list, all the words in each group contain the same sound. Notice that one sound can have several different spellings, e.g. /ʌ/ young, but, company. Listen carefully to the pronunciation of each word and repeat it.

/ʌ/	/ɪ/	/i:/	/ʊ/	/u:/
discuss	finish	keen	put	suit
customer	event	clean	look	recruit
production	trip	cheap	goods	move
study	image	easy	full	lose
company	manage	medium	took	include
government	market	receive	push	choose
worry	budget	scheme	could	group
young	business	reason	woman	through

/ju:/	/ɑ:/	/ɔ:/	/ɜ:/	/eə/
useful	start	door	were	where
refuse	calm	report	purchase	share
excuse	fast	course	turnover	careful
due	sharply	call	merge	parent
opportunity	staff	law	learn	prepare
produce	demand	ordinary	worth	area
huge	plant	automatic	reserve	chairman
future	heart	cause	firm	wear

/aɪ/	/eɪ/	/əʊ/	/aʊ/	/ə/	/ə/
buy	main	most	now	about	normal
kind	save	whole	allow	agree	important
sign	based	bonus	account	available	total
finance	train	chosen	discount	propose	person
private	latest	known	output	opinion	doctor
supply	danger	borrow	found	commission	worker
finally	delay	loan	powerful	control	camera
client	sale	local	shower	suggest	agent

NOTE: This list follows standard British English pronunciation.

Diagnostic Grammar Test

Do this test to find out which areas of grammar you need to work on. You can check your answers in the key on page125. This page also tells you where you can find an explanation of each grammar point.

Complete each sentence in the most natural way. Sometimes one word is necessary, sometimes you will need two or even three words. Read each sentence carefully before you write.

e.g. John _can't_ speak French, but he can speak German.

1. Sony _____ electronic equipment.
2. He _____ in Paris at the moment.
3. _____ does it cost?
4. Can I borrow _____ money?
5. _____ three secretaries in the sales department.
6. _____ you like to come to the cinema this evening?
7. _____ Anna Gordon, our financial controller, before?
8. I am sorry I can't come. I _____ dinner with a client this evening.
9. The factory is very old. It _____ in 1952.
10. We must contact him before he _____.
11. I went to the supermarket _____ some bread.
12. I want _____ discuss this with me before we make a decision.
13. He left the office five _____.
14. Maria Martinez? Yes, I know her very _____.
15. Tokyo is _____ than Paris.
16. How _____ he travel to the U.S.? About once a month.
17. When _____ we meet? How about 6:30?
18. _____ give this fax to John, please?
19. If I _____ his phone number, I would call him.
20. _____ lunch, we went for a walk in the park.
21. I'm sorry. What _____ say?
22. If you don't like London you _____ move to the country.
23. Bye. _____ see you on Friday.
24. I enjoyed the book because _____ so different.
25. She _____ have to work with him. She wanted to.
26. He _____ for us since 1988.
27. The Nile is _____ river in the world.
28. Next year we _____ to launch three new products.
29. _____ a post office near here?
30. If they offer you the job, _____ you take it?

Grammar Reference and Practice

CONTENTS

	Page		Page
THE PRESENT	82	EXERCISE 5	97
Present Simple	82		
There is.../There are...	83	**too** and **enough**	97
Present Continuous	84	Comparison of Adjectives	99
EXERCISE 1	85		
		COUNTABLE AND	101
THE FUTURE	86	UNCOUNTABLE	
will	86	Nouns	101
going to	87	**some** and **any**	101
Present Continuous	87	**how much? how many?**	102
		a little and **a few**	
THE PAST	88	EXERCISE 6	102
Past Simple	88		
Present Perfect	89	THE ARTICLE	103
EXERCISE 2	90	**a** and **some**	103
		the	103
IF SENTENCES	90	No Article	104
1st Conditional	90	EXERCISE 7	104
2nd Conditional	91		
		PERSONAL PRONOUNS	104
THE PASSIVE	92	AND ADJECTIVES	
EXERCISE 3	92	Pronouns	105
		Possessives	105
MODAL VERBS	93	**each other**	105
must, have to,	94	EXERCISE 8	106
and **need to**			
can and **could**	94	THE INFINITIVE	106
shall	95	Infinitive of Purpose	106
should and **ought to**	95	**would like** and **want**	106
EXERCISE 4	95		
		Key to Diagnostic	125
ADJECTIVES AND ADVERBS	96	Grammar Test	
Adjectives	96		
Adverbs	96	Key to Grammar	125
		Exercises	

The Present

PRESENT SIMPLE

Infinitive:	**to be**		
I	am		[I'm]
You/we/they	are	French.	[You're/we're/they're]
He/she/it	is		[He's/she's/it's]

Question: Am I?　　Are you/we/they?　　Is he/she/it?

Negative: I am not.　　You/we/they are not [aren't].　　He/she/it is not [isn't].

Infinitive:	**to have**		
I/you/we/they	have	a French name.	[I've/you've/we've/they've (got)]
He/she/it	has		[He's/she's/it's (got)]

Question: Have I/you/we/they (got) an Italian name?
Has he/she/it (got) an Italian name?
OR: Do I/you/we/they have? Does he/she/it have?

Negative: I/you/we/they have not [haven't] (got) a German name.
He/she/it has not [hasn't] (got) a German name.
OR: I/you/we/they do not [don't] have a Spanish name.
He/she/it does not [doesn't] have a Spanish name.

NOTE: **have got** is common in spoken British English.

Infinitive:	**to work**	
I/you/we/they	work	very fast.
He/she/it	works	

Question: Do I/you/we/they work slowly?　　Does he/she/it work slowly?

Negative: I/you/we/they do not [don't] work.　　He/she/it does not [doesn't] work.

USES

General time: To talk about things which are true now and which we don't expect to change, i.e. things which are not temporary.

e.g. *I live in London.*
Ford makes cars.

Repeated actions: To talk about things we do repeatedly or regularly (often with words like never, often, sometimes, etc.).

e.g. *She sometimes takes sugar with her coffee.*
I have meetings with my manager twice a month.

PRACTICE

Look at the pictures and talk about Tom's daily routine. Begin like this: *"He gets up at 7 o'clock..."*

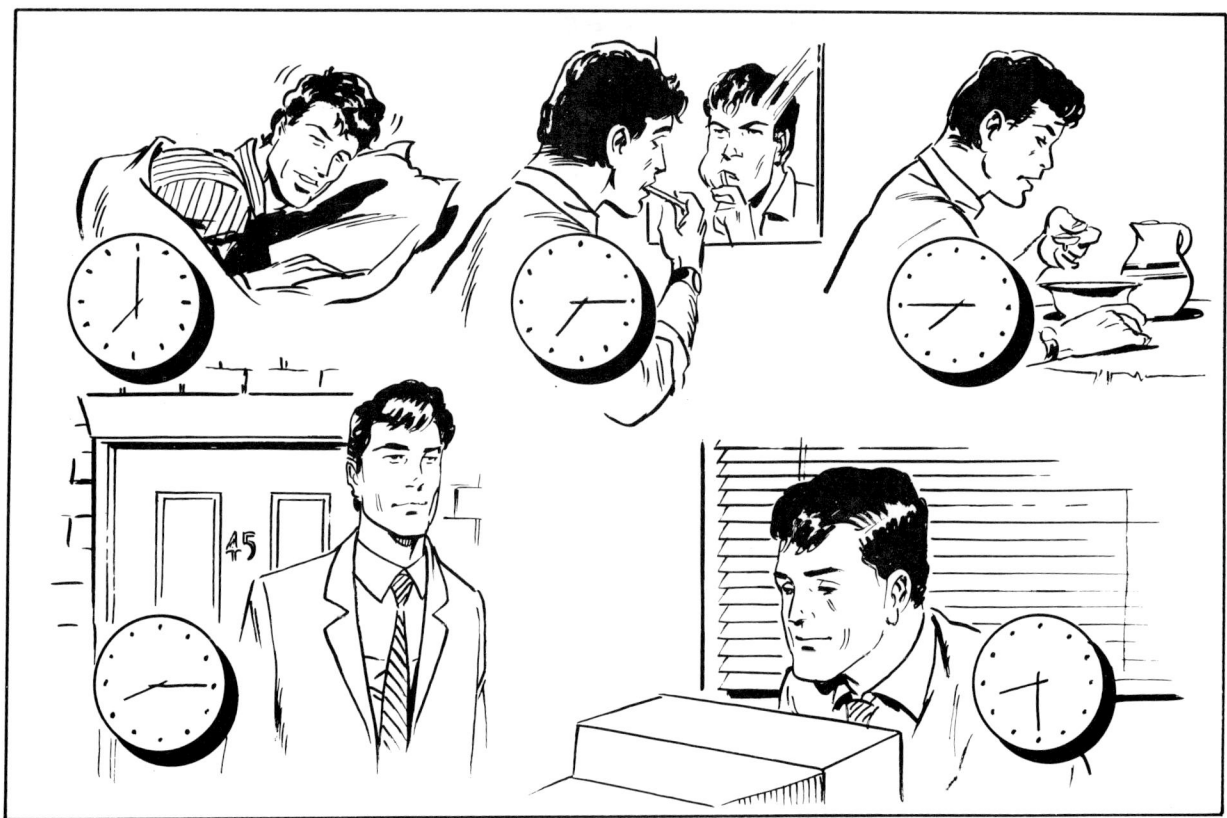

THERE IS.../THERE ARE...

There is	a good film	on TV tonight.	[There's]
are	two good films		

USES

Existence: To talk about the existence of something.

e.g. *There is a restaurant in Ock Street.* (<u>not</u> *A restaurant is in...*)
There are four representatives for Spain. (<u>not</u> *Four reps are...*)

PRACTICE

Look at the picture and talk about the things you see in the room. Begin like this: *"There are two paintings on the wall..."*

PRESENT CONTINUOUS

Infinitive:	**to be** + **-ing**		
I	am		[I'm]
You/we/they	are	waiting.	[You're/we're/they're]
He/she/it	is		[He's/she's/it's]

Question: Am I waiting?   Are you/we/they waiting?   Is he/she/it waiting?

Negative: I am not waiting. You/we/they are not [aren't] waiting.
He/she/it is not [isn't] waiting.

USES

Now: To talk about actions or events which are happening now.

e.g. *He is waiting for you in reception.*

Developments: To talk about things which are changing at the moment.

e.g. *The company is expanding.*

Temporary: To talk about actions or events which are not permanent.

e.g. *I am dealing with her letters while she is away.*

PRACTICE

Look at the pictures and say what the people are doing.

e.g. *Three people are waiting for a bus.*

EXERCISE 1

Compare: *I design buildings (that's my job).*
    and: *I am designing a new shopping centre (that's my current project).*

Put the verbs into the correct form: present simple or present continuous.

e.g. She *is preparing* (prepare) the figures for next week's meeting.

1. Can you turn that radio off? I _____ (try) to work.
2. The post _____ (not/come) before 8:30 a.m.
3. She knows a lot about politics. She _____ (read) the newspaper every morning.
4. I _____ (read) a very interesting book. It's about Quality Circles.
5. Which hand _____ (you/write) with?
6. Two capuccinos, please. Sorry, sir we _____ (not/serve) coffee.
7. Can I speak to Mr Tanner, please? I am sorry. He _____ (not/work) this week. He is on holiday.
8. The quality of their products _____ (improve) rapidly.

The Future

WILL

will + infinitive without **to**

I/you/he/she/it/we/they	will go	tomorrow.	[I'll/you'll/he'll/she'll/it'll/we'll/they'll]

Question: Will I/you/he/she/it/we/they go tomorrow?

Negative: I/you/he/she/it/we/they will not [won't] go tomorrow.

NOTE: **shall** is sometimes used as the first person of **will**, particularly in British English.

e.g. *I/we shall probably know his answer very soon.*

USES

Instant decision: When we decide on a future action and speak at the moment of deciding.

e.g. *I can't tell you now. I'll tell you tomorrow.*
I'm busy now but I'll call you back in half an hour.

Prediction: To say what we think will happen in the future (often with verbs like think, expect, hope, etc.).

e.g. *I think they will wait until next year.*
I hope it will be all right.
Perhaps she will listen to you.

Statement of fact: To talk about certainties or make a promise.

e.g. *The bus will leave at 8:15 tomorrow morning.*
Some things will never change.
Don't worry. I won't be late.

PRACTICE

Talk about next year. (What year will it be?) Give some facts and make some predictions.

e.g. *Next year, the company will be five years old.*
I expect it will be another good year for us.

GOING TO

Infinitive: **to be going to** + infinitive

I	am		
You/we/they	are	going to	arrive in time.
He/she/it	is		

Question: Am I going to arrive in time? Are you/we/they going to arrive in time?
Is he/she/it going to arrive in time?

Negative: I am not going to arrive in time.
You/we/they are not going to arrive in time.
He/she/it is not going to arrive in time.

USES

Intentions: When we have decided or when we plan to do something.

e.g. *I am going to stop smoking.*
They are going to find a new supplier.

Prediction: When we can see clearly that a thing will happen.

e.g. *Be careful! That chair is going to fall over.*
There's going to be an increase in the price of oil.

PRACTICE

Make some New Year's resolutions (to be a better person).

e.g. *I am going to do more exercise.*
I am going to work harder.

PRESENT CONTINUOUS

USES

Arrangements: When an action is fixed or arranged.

e.g. *I am flying to Scotland tomorrow.*
We are meeting him outside the cinema at 7 o'clock.

PRACTICE

Look at the diary and say what John's arrangements are. Begin like this:
"He is having lunch with Peter on Friday at 1 p.m."

The Past

PAST SIMPLE

infinitive + -ed

I/you/he/she/it/we/they	helped.
Question:	Did I/you/he/she/it/we/they help?
Negative:	I/you/he/she/it/we/they did not [didn't] help.

NOTE: use – used   try – tried   stop – stopped
            like – liked   apply – applied   ban – banned

There are many verbs which are not regular. A list of these can be found on page 126, but here are are a few of the important ones.

have – had   go – went   give – gave   come – came
take – took   be – was/were   make – made   say – said
send – sent   put – put   tell – told   think - thought

USES

Finished actions: To talk about events which happened in the past and are finished (either single events or things which happened one after the other).

e.g. *She telephoned me yesterday.*

I didn't enjoy the film. It was too violent.

He got up, washed, and went downstairs. There was a letter by the door. He picked it up and went into the kitchen.

PRACTICE

Make sentences about things you did at these times.

e.g. *Last night I worked late at the office.*

Last night   Three days ago   When I was six
In 1990   Yesterday   Last weekend

PRESENT PERFECT

have + past participle

I/you/we/they	have	arrived now.	[I've/you've/we've/they've]
He/she/it	has		[He's/she's/it's]

Question: Have I/you/we/they used it before?   Has he/she/it arrived yet?

Negative: I/you/we/they have not [haven't] used it before.
He/she/it has not [hasn't] arrived yet.

USES

Indefinite time: To talk about something which happened in the past, when we do not fix the time that it happened. If we say, or suggest, the time it happened, then we must use the past simple.

> e.g. *She has worked with children before.*
> *I have seen that film too.*
> *Have you ever been to Spain?*
> but *We met at John's party.* (not *We have met...*)

Unfinished time: To refer to a time which is not finished even though the action or event may be finished.

> e.g. *He has worked here since 1988. (He works here now.)*
> *He worked here for 12 years. (He does not work here now.)*
> *She has written over 30 books. (She is a living writer.)*
> *She wrote over 30 books. (She is dead or no longer a writer.)*
> *They have visited five countries this year. They visited five countries last year.*

Recent time: When the event is in the recent past and has more relevance to the present than to the past.

> e.g. *Your taxi has arrived. (It is waiting outside.)*
> *I've mended the car. (It works now.)*

Compare and *I fell off a horse when I was six and broke my leg.*
A *I fell off a horse yesterday.*
B *Are you O.K.?*
A *No, I've broken my leg.*

PRACTICE

Use the present perfect to answer these questions. Each time begin like this:
"I don't know. I..."

e.g. *Where is Paul? I don't know. I haven't seen him.*

What do you think of this book?
Do you like Turkish coffee?
Is it a good restaurant?
Is Chinese a difficult language to learn?
How does this machine work?
Is she an interesting person?

EXERCISE 2

Put the verbs into the correct form: past simple or present perfect.

e.g. Yes, I know Kate. We *have been* (be) friends for a long time.

1. I'm sorry, I can't tell you. They _____ (not/publish) the results. I will call you as soon as I know.
2. I _____ (go) on holiday with her last year.
3. The sales figures for this month are excellent. We _____ (sell) over 30,000 units.
4. I _____ (work) on many interesting projects for them, but I think this is the most exciting.
5. No, she _____ (not/leave) the company. She's on holiday.
6. Do you remember what _____ (happen) to Jane when she went to that dentist?

If Sentences

1ST CONDITIONAL

If + present simple, _____ **will** _____.

If she gets the job, she will be very happy.

NOTE: We also use this sentence structure with **when, after, until, as soon as, before**, etc.

e.g. *I will tell him when I see him.*
We will wait until he arrives.

USES

Real situations: To talk about something real and possible (in the present or future).

e.g. *Situation:*   *It is 5:20 p.m. and the next train leaves at 6:00 p.m.*
It takes 30 minutes to get to the station.

Conditional Sentence: If we leave now, we'll catch the 6:00 train.

Situation: You want to buy a new car, but the seller is asking too much.

Conditional Sentence: If he reduces the price, I'll buy it.

PRACTICE

Read what will happen if Tom goes out tonight and continue the sequence with similar sentences.

I'm sorry, I can't go out tonight. If I go out, I will go to bed late. If I go to bed late, I will not wake up in the morning. If I don't wake up in the morning, I...

2ND CONDITIONAL

If + past simple, _____ **would** _____.

If I knew the answer, I would tell you.

NOTE: With the verb **be**, use **were** <u>not</u> **was**.

e.g. *If I were you, I would accept their offer.*
     If she were here, she would be able to tell you.

USES

Imaginary situations: To talk about situations which are unreal or hypothetical (in the present or future).

e.g. *If I spoke Portuguese, I would apply for the job in Brazil. (I don't speak Portuguese.)*
    If she had a bigger car, she would take us. (Her car is too small.)

Improbabilities: To talk about things which are possible, but not very likely/probable.

e.g. *I would be very surprised if he came. (He probably won't come.)*
    If it rained, we would cancel the trip. (It probably won't rain.)

PRACTICE

Look at these situations and say what you would do.

What would you do if...

...you saw someone stealing a car?
...you found $500 in the street?
...a stranger asked you to lend him $75?
...you could be the leader of your country for a day?

The Passive

> **be** + past participle
>
> They are built in Japan.
> It was built in 1962 by Richard Rogers.
>
> NOTE: The participle never changes. To change the tense, change
>   the verb **be**.
>
> | | |
> |---|---|
> | Present Simple: | The office is painted every year. |
> | Present Continuous: | The office is being painted at the moment. |
> | Present Perfect: | The office has been painted. |
> | Past Simple: | The office was painted last week. |
> | **will**: | The office will be painted next week. |
> | **going to**: | The office is going to be painted next week. |
> | **can/must/should**: | The office can/must/should be painted soon. |

USES

No agent: When we don't need or want to say who did the action.

e.g. *The man was arrested last night.* (<u>not</u> *The police arrested...*)
     He has been promoted to manager. (<u>not</u> *The company has promoted...*)
     Tomatoes are grown in this area. (<u>not</u> *Farmers grow tomatoes...*)

Giving facts: When we are concentrating on one thing and are describing what happens
                 or happened to it.

e.g. *The Sistine chapel is in the Vatican. It was built by Sixtus IV in the fifteenth
     century. Later, parts of it were painted by Michaelangelo...*

EXERCISE 3

Put the verb into the passive. Make sure you use the right form of the verb
be (was, has been, should be, is being, etc.).

e.g. Why didn't you bring your car today?
     It *is being repaired* (repair).

1. Where is your calculator?
   It _____ (steal).
2. Why did Brian leave?
   He didn't leave. He _____ (fire).
3. When will I know if I have got the job?
   You _____ (tell) tomorrow.

4. What is the best way to send this letter?

   It _____ (fax).

5. What do you do with the jeans that have defects in them?

   They _____ (sell) at a discount.

6. Has the management decided what to do with the old cafeteria?

   Yes, it _____ (close) down.

Modal Verbs

modal verb + infinitive without **to**

I/you/he/she/it/we/they	can could will would shall should must	work better.

Question:	Can I help?	Could you come?	Will he pay?	Would she agree?
	Should it go?	Shall we see?	Must they know?	

Negative: I cannot [can't] tell you. You could not [couldn't] come.
He will not [won't] come. She would not [wouldn't] pay.
It should not [shouldn't] go. We shall not [shan't] pay.
They must not [mustn't] know.

ought to + infinitive

I/you/he/she/it/we/they	ought to	stay there.

Question: Ought I/you/he/she/it/we/they to stay there?

Negative: I/you/he/she/it/we/they ought not [oughtn't] to stay there.

have to + infinitive
need to

I/you/we/they	have to need to	speak to him.
He/she/it	has to needs to	work better.

Question:	Do I/you/we/they have to speak to him?
	Does he/she/it have to be ready this afternoon?
	Do I/you/we/they need to speak to her?
	Does he/she/it need to be ready this afternoon?
Negative:	I/you/we/they do not [don't] have to visit the client on Friday.
	He/she/it does not [doesn't] have to wait.
	I/you/we/they do not [don't] need to stay late.
	He/she/it does not [doesn't] need to be ready by 5 p.m.
OR:	I/you/he/she/it/we/they need not [needn't] stay late.

USES

MUST, HAVE TO AND NEED TO

Obligation: To say there is an obligation to do something, we use **must**. To say there is an obligation <u>not</u> to do something, we use **must not**.

e.g. *I must remember to post those letters.*
You mustn't smoke in the elevator.
We must not be late.

Have to is like **must** but we use it when the obligation comes from outside, from someone else.

e.g. *In Japan people have to drive on the left. (The law says so.)*
She has to start work at 8 a.m. (Her company says so.)

Necessity: To say there is a necessity to do something, we use **need to**.

e.g. *I need to buy a new battery for my watch.*
He needs to speak to you today.

No obligation: To say there is no obligation, we use **not have to** and **not need to**.

e.g. *You don't have to answer that question, if you don't want to.*
He's very rich. He doesn't need to work.

CAN AND COULD

Ability: To say that someone or something has the ability or capacity to do something, we use **can** (in the present) and **could** (in the past).

e.g. *She can speak four languages.*
I could ski when I was five years old.
This train can go at 300 kph.

Requests: To ask for permission to do something or ask another person to do it we use **could** or **can**. **Could** is a little more polite than **can**.

e.g. *Can you tell me your name?*

Could I open a window? It's very hot in here.

Possibility: To say that it is possible for someone to do something, we use **could** or **can**. To say that it is possible that something will happen, we use **could** but <u>not</u> **can**.

e.g. *We can/could talk about that another time.*

She could/can meet you on Tuesday.

Don't wait for me. I could be late. (<u>not</u> I can be late.)

It could be a difficult meeting. (<u>not</u> It can be a difficult...)

SHALL

Suggestions: In British English, to suggest a particular action we can make a question with **shall** (but only with 'I' and 'we)'.

e.g. *Shall I come to your house or will you come to mine?*

Shall we have lunch together before the meeting?

SHOULD AND OUGHT TO

Right and wrong: We use **should** and **ought to** to say what is the right thing to do and **shouldn't** and, in British English, **oughtn't to** for the wrong thing.

e.g. *You shouldn't leave your car unlocked.*

They ought to listen to his advice.

You should lie down if you are not feeling well.

We oughtn't to waste time on this project.

EXERCISE 4

Choose the correct word(s) to complete these sentences.

e.g. When _____ be at the airport?

a) you must   (b) do you have to   c) mustn't you

1. I _____ to go to Vienna next month.
   a) have   b) needn't   c) must
2. Club members _____ pay.
   a) mustn't   b) doesn't need to   c) don't have to
3. You _____ worry about me. I'll be all right.
   a) must   b) needn't   c) doesn't need to
4. You have written my name wrong. It _____ have two m's.
   a) should   b) could   c) would

5. If you ran every day like me, you _____ be healthy.

   a) can　　　　　　　b) will　　　　　　　c) would

6. Mr Brown is waiting in reception. _____ I ask him to come up?

   a) shall　　　　　　b) will　　　　　　　c) would

7. You _____ not to eat so much. You will get fat.

   a) could　　　　　　b) ought　　　　　　c) should

8. The strike at the car plant _____ go on for a long time.

   a) could　　　　　　b) ought　　　　　　c) can

Adjectives and Adverbs

ADJECTIVES

An adjective describes or complements a noun. In English the adjective comes before <u>not</u> after the noun, and its form never changes.

e.g. *He is good.*
That is an interesting idea.
We visited some interesting places on our holiday.

ADVERBS

adjective + **-ly**

badly, interestingly, cheaply, honestly

NOTE:　happy – happily　　funny – funnily　　lucky – luckily

There are also some irregular adverbs.

good　–　well
hard　–　hard
fast　–　fast

USES

Manner:　Adverbs of manner describe how an action is done (quickly, well, quietly, etc.) and come after the main verb and its direct object if it has one.

e.g. *He drives slowly.*
I look carefully in both directions when I cross the road.
Our agent speaks English fluently (<u>not</u> speaks fluently English).
I know Spain well (<u>not</u> know well Spain).
She likes jazz music very much (<u>not</u> likes very much jazz).

Frequency: Adverbs of frequency describe how often an action is done (sometimes, often, never, etc.). They usually come before the main verb, but after if the verb is **be**.

e.g. *I usually do the shopping on Saturdays.*
He rarely gives interviews.

but *She is often in London on business.*

PRACTICE

Make sentences about yourself using the adverbs below.

e.g. *I am never late for appointments. I play tennis very well.*

never	sometimes	always	often
slowly	very well	fast	carefully

EXERCISE 5

Look at these sentences and say if they are right or wrong.

e.g. She is a very nice person. Right
I like very much skiing. Wrong

1. Believe me. It is her really name. _____
2. We have lived always in Toulon. _____
3. I know exactly what you mean. _____
4. They produce cars cheaply. _____
5. She is working hard at the moment. _____
6. I think your idea is well. _____
7. I don't often worry about money. _____
8. He wears a uniform black and gold. _____

TOO AND ENOUGH

too + adjective/adverb to do a thing.
for a thing.

She is too young to get married.

(**not**) + adjective/adverb + **enough** to do a thing.
for a thing.

She is (not) old enough for the job.

USES

too: We use **too** to mean **more than is good**. If you only want to make the adjective or adverb stronger, use **very**.

> e.g. *The course was too long.*
> *The course was very interesting (<u>not</u> too interesting).*
> *He speaks too quickly for me.*
> *He speaks very clearly (<u>not</u> too clearly).*

(not)...enough: We use **(not)...enough** to say that something is satisfactory or unsatisfactory in some way.

> e.g. *The room is big enough for 40 people.*
> *The machine does not work fast enough.*
> *I am not tall enough to reach the light. I need a ladder.*

PRACTICE

Look at the pictures and make sentences using **too** and **(not)...enough**.

e.g. *He is too tired to work.*

COMPARISON OF ADJECTIVES

	Adjective	Comparative	Superlative
One syllable	big	bigger	the biggest
	old	older	the oldest
	rich	richer	the richest
Two syllables	pretty	prettier	the prettiest
	quiet	quieter	the quietest
	tiring	more tiring	the most tiring
Three or more syllables	beautiful	more beautiful	the most beautiful
	expensive	more expensive	the most expensive
	serious	more serious	the most serious
NOTE:	good	better	the best
	bad	worse	the worst
	many	more	the most
	a little	less	the least

With two-syllable adjectives sometimes **-er** is correct, sometimes **more** and sometimes either. But usually after adjectives which end in **-ive, -ed, -ing, -ish,** and **-ful**, we use **more** and **the most**.

For adjectives which end in **-y**, and **-ly**, change the **-y** to an **-i** and add **-er** or **-est**.

USES

Comparatives: To compare two things.

e.g. *The bus is cheaper than the train.*
Squash is more tiring than tennis.
France is nice, but I think Spain is nicer.

Superlatives: To say that one thing is **more (...) than** all the others.

e.g. *Mount Everest is the highest mountain in the world.*
We are the most famous pharmaceutical company in Europe.

PRACTICE

Compare the things you see in the pictures.

e.g. *Number 1 is the most comfortable car.*

1

2

3

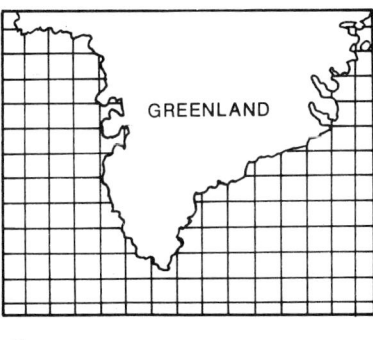

4

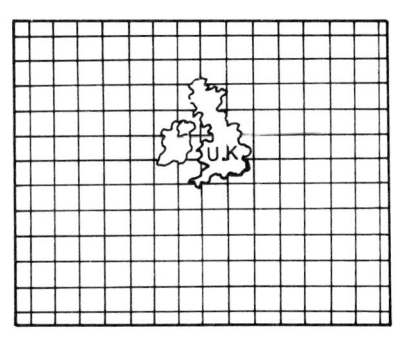

5

6

7

8

9

Countable and Uncountable

NOUNS

Some nouns are countable.   e.g. *girl, town, machine*
Some nouns are uncountable.   e.g. *butter, information, money*

Countable nouns have a singular and a plural form.

girl	girls
town	towns
machine	machines

NOTE: There are some irregular plurals.

woman	women	foot	feet
person	people	child	children

Uncountable nouns only have one form.
butter
information
money

A test you can use to know if a noun is uncountable is to say to yourself, "Can I say seven girls?" (yes), "Can I say seven moneys?" (no).

Here are some common uncountable nouns.

advice	cash	money	fun
staff	equipment	mail	news
progress	furniture	work	research

SOME AND ANY

USES

Statements: Generally we use **some** for affirmative statements and **any** for negative statements.

    e.g. *I have some money in the bank.*
        I don't have any money in the bank.
        There are some chairs in the other room.
        There aren't any chairs in the other room.

Questions: We use **any** in questions when we do not expect a particular answer (the answer could be either **yes** or **no**). We use **some** when we expect, or hope for, the answer **yes**.

e.g. *Are there any women in the Swiss army?*

Could you give me some information about flights to Japan?

HOW MUCH? HOW MANY? A LITTLE AND A FEW

USES

Quantity: There are some expressions of quantity which are used with countable nouns and some with uncountable nouns.

e.g. *I have a few details about the house.*

I have a little information about the house.

How much milk do you want in your tea?

How many spoons of sugar do you want in your tea?

but *He gave me a lot of good advice.*

He gave me a lot of good reasons for his decision.

PRACTICE

Go to your next-door-neighbour to borrow the things below. Ask questions like: "*Could I borrow some milk?*" The neighbour will say things like: "*I only have a little*" or "*How much do you need?*".

sugar   eggs   oil   glasses   a lemon   butter

EXERCISE 6

Choose the best answer to complete each sentence.

e.g. I'm going to invest some _____ in property.
 a) moneys   (b) money   c) dollar

1. I'd like to take _____ photographs. Is that O.K.?
  a) some   b) any   c) a
2. I'm sorry. There are _____ flights to Portland today.
  a) some   b) any   c) no
3. How _____ people work in your department?
  a) much   b) many   c) little
4. I only have _____ tickets for tonight's performance.
  a) a little   b) a few   c) a lot of
5. It has _____ interesting features, but I don't like the design.
  a) a little   b) a few of   c) a lot of
6. There is _____ I want to tell you. I'm getting married.
  a) something   b) anything   c) nothing
7. You have done a good _____ for us and we are very grateful.
  a) job   b) jobs   c) work

8. There is a lot of _____ here and I need time to study it.

   a) facts   b) information   c) informations

The Article

	Indefinite Article	Definite Article
Singular	a (car)	the (car)
Plural	some (cars)	the (cars)
Uncountable	some (paper)	the (paper)

USES

A AND SOME

First mention: To refer to something or somebody for the first time.

e.g. *He works for a small company near Oxford.*
There are some very old houses in the town centre.

One of many: To refer to a thing in general (one of many), not a particular thing.

e.g. *I am looking for a new car.*
Do you have a pen that I could borrow?

THE

Particular things: To refer to a particular thing/person or the only thing/person in a particular context.

e.g. *The pub in Marston Street is not very comfortable.*
The sales manager is 43 years old.

Second mention: When the listener already knows what it is that we are talking about.

e.g. *He lives in a small house in a village in the south of Spain. The village is also quite small.*
She gave me a pen and some paper, but the pen didn't work.

NOTE: the country, the sea, the air
              the piano, the guitar, the violin
              the radio, the cinema, the television

e.g. *We lived in London for 15 years, but now we have moved to the country.*
She plays the piano very well.
Yes, I heard the news on the radio this morning.

NO ARTICLE

Generalizing: To make a general statement about something.

e.g. *Cows eat grass.*
War is evil.
Women are more careful drivers than men.

NOTE: dinner, lunch, breakfast
home, school, university

e.g. *I met him for lunch yesterday.*
John's still at school and Sarah is going to university this year.

EXERCISE 7

Complete each sentence with **a, the, some,** or nothing.

e.g. After _____ breakfast, I go for *a* run.

1. Please write your name and nationality at _____ top of the paper.
2. I love to swim in _____ sea, but I don't like _____ swimming pools.
3. Have you seen _____ small brown dog? I've lost him.
4. _____ moon is very bright tonight.
5. _____ people say that _____ experience in selling is less important than knowledge of the product.
6. After _____ cup of coffee in _____ cafe opposite the theatre I went home.

Personal Pronouns and Adjectives

Subject	Object	Possessive Adjective	Possessive Pronoun
I	me	my	mine
you	you	your	yours
he	him	his	his
she	her	her	hers
it	it	its	its
we	us	our	ours
you (pl.)	you	your	yours
they	them	their	theirs

USES

PRONOUNS

Personal pronouns cannot usually be left out.

> e.g. I didn't buy the car because <u>it</u> was too expensive.
> He is rich, but <u>he</u> is also very generous.
> They are old and I think we should replace <u>them</u>.

Substitution: We use these pronouns in place of a noun, <u>not</u> as well as a noun.

> e.g. My wife is a doctor <u>or</u> She is a doctor. (<u>not</u> My wife she is a doctor.)
> The plan worked very well <u>or</u> It worked very well. (<u>not</u> The plan it worked very well.)

Object pronouns: The object pronoun can be direct or indirect.

> e.g. He wrote a letter to me last week.
> I told them to wait outside.

NOTE: **them** can refer to people or things.

> e.g. Where are my glasses? I put them in the drawer.
> Where are the children? I saw them in the garden five minutes ago.

POSSESSIVES

We use the possessive adjective before a noun and the possessive pronoun without a noun (because the noun is already known).

> e.g. Is this your pen? Yes, it's mine. (Yes, it's my pen.)
> Where do the Smiths live? Their house is next to ours. (Their house is next to our house.)

EACH OTHER

We use **each other** when we want to say that two people do the same action and the object of the action is the other person.

> e.g. They love each other very much. (She loves him and he loves her.)
> They agreed with each other on most things.
> We talked to each other for hours.

EXERCISE 8

Complete the passage using the right pronoun or possessive adjective.

When John asked me to go on holiday with _____ to Norway, I thought _____ was a good idea and _____ agreed. It was only when _____ arrived in Nordkapp three weeks later with _____ tent that I realized _____ mistake. _____ was -18 C and the days were only four hours long. We had warm clothes with _____, but no proper sleeping bags. John's sleeping bag was quite new, but _____ was 20 years old.

The Infinitive

to do
to be, to work, to say
Negative: **not to do**

USES

INFINITIVE OF PURPOSE

To say why someone does something.

NOTE: We can't use **not to do** in this way.

e.g. *He went to Paris to visit his sister.*
I'm meeting her tomorrow to talk about the situation.

WOULD LIKE AND WANT

After **would like** and **want**.

e.g. *Would you like to sit down for a moment?*
I would like you to come with me to Hawaii.
He wants to speak to the manager.
Do you want me to call him?

PRACTICE

You have a new robot to help you in the office. Give it some instructions.

e.g. *First I want you to answer these letters. Then I would like you to...*

1 A PERSONAL PRESENTATION

PROFILE OF A COMPANY CHAIRMAN

He is very rich but he lives like an ordinary person.

For a company chairman he is also very young.

COUNTRIES AND NATIONALITIES

Nationality	Language	Currency
Australian	English	Dollar
Belgian	French/Flemish	Franc
Spanish	Spanish	Peseta
Kuwaiti	Arabic	Dinar
Canadian	English/French	Dollar
Mexican	Spanish	Peso
Chinese	Chinese	Yuan
Italian	Italian	Lira
Singaporean	Chinese/Malay/ English	Dollar
Danish	Danish	Krone

2 A JOB DESCRIPTION

WHO DOES WHAT?

Administrative Staff	Sales Staff
arrange appointments	present new products
type letters	negotiate agreements
attend meetings	deal with inquiries
answer the phone	visit clients
	discuss marketing strategy
	attend meetings

A VISIT TO A COMPANY

PR Officer	...so, I do hope you found that interesting.
Daniel	Yes, very.
PR Officer	Good, well I suggest we go and have a coffee in the cafeteria. That will give you a chance to meet some of the others.
Daniel	Great. I'd like that.
PR Officer	John, I'd like you to meet Daniel Carne. He's from CDC.
John	How do you do?
Daniel	Pleased to meet you, John.
PR Officer	John's our production foreman. He supervises the assembly workers and makes sure that all the machines are in good working order. Tea or coffee?
Daniel	Coffee, please. Black with sugar.
PR Officer	Here you are. Ah, and this is Louise Fairchild and Maggie Stewart. Louise is from personnel. She's responsible for recruiting and training new staff, and Maggie handles all our special accounts.
Daniel	Oh, I see. Finance.
Maggie	Well, no actually. I'm part of the sales team. I negotiate agreements with large retailers.
Daniel	Right.
PR Officer	And this is David Baird, our export sales manager.
Daniel	Nearly half your sales are exports, aren't they? Um... Which countries do you deal with?
David	Well, I have to travel to most countries in northern Europe. And about once a month I meet all the reps from the other areas like North Africa, Italy, the Middle East and so on.

1. John, Production. Supervises staff.
2. Louise, Personnel. Trains staff.
3. Maggie, Sales. Negotiates.
4. David, Export Sales. Travels and attends meetings.

A JOB DESCRIPTION

A civil engineer builds roads, bridges, dams, etc.

An auditor checks company accounts.

A tax consultant advises people about tax problems.

An air traffic controller monitors flights.

A solicitor deals with legal problems and advises clients.

A copywriter designs and writes advertisements.

A medical research assistant researches new drugs.

A public relations officer is responsible for a company's image and deals with customers and journalists.

A maintenance engineer repairs and services machines.

An equity trader buys and sells shares.

COMPANY ORGANIZATION

1. Production Foreman
2. Health & Safety
3. Export Sales Manager
4. Stores & Transport
5. Company Training Manager
6. Marketing Director
7. Advertising & Sales Promotion Manager
8. Development Manager
9. Chief Accountant
10. Production Director

3 A BUSINESS TRIP

SPELLING

/eɪ/	as in day	A H J K
/iː/	as in me	B C D E G P T V (Z)
/e/	as in pen	F L M N S X Z
/aɪ/	as in why	I Y
/uː/	as in blue	Q U W
/əʊ/	as in phone	O
/ɑː/	as in car	R

COMPANY NAMES

Stockbroker Here is a list of six leading multinationals which we feel are good, low risk investments for you to consider. I'll read them to you.

First there's Exxon, the oil and gas company, with a turnover of $47.5 billion a year. That's Exxon, E-X-X-O-N. Second, another American company, Sears Roebuck. Its turnover is $38 billion a year. That's Sears, S-E-A-R-S, Roebuck, R-O-E-B-U-C-K. Then the Japanese company, Mitsubishi, M-I-T-S-U-B-I-S-H-I. Its turnover is $57.4 billion. Fourth is the tobacco giant, Philip Morris. That's Morris, M-O-R-R-I-S. Turnover $20 billion. And the last two are European companies: E.N.I. of Italy, turnover $14.2 billion, and Unilever, U.K. and the Netherlands, turnover $17 billion. That's Unilever, U-N-I-L-E-V-E-R.

Name	Turnover (U.S. $bn)
Sears Roebuck	38
Mitsubishi	57.4
Philip Morris	20
E.N.I.	14.2
Unilever	17

REQUESTING

Visitor	Excuse me, I'm lost. Can you tell me which floor Mr Maxwell's office is on?
Employee	Yes, of course. It's on the fifth floor.
Visitor	Thank you very much.
Cashier	Yes, can I help you?
Customer	Yes. I'm going to Switzerland next week. Could you transfer $2000 to my account in Zurich.
Cashier	Certainly. Can I have your name and account number, please?
Francesca	Hello. It's Francesca here. Listen, my train is going to be one hour late. Could you possibly phone Chris Weber and cancel my appointment with him?
Secretary	Sure. Do you want me to fix another time?
Francesca	No, that's O.K. Just tell him I'm very sorry.

1. visitor and employee (i.e. strangers), customer and cashier, two colleagues
2. an office building, a bank, on the telephone
3. Mr Maxwell's office, to transfer $2000 to Zurich, to cancel an appointment

A BUSINESS TRIP

1. book/arrange
2. send
3. cancel/reserve/book
4. find out
5. arrange/fix/change/cancel
6. borrow
7. let Ken know

ASKING FOR HELP (possible answers)

1. Excuse me. Could you tell me the way to the Hyatt Regency Hotel?
2. Could you change these U.S. dollars for Hong Kong dollars?
3. Could I have a newspaper with my breakfast, please?
4. Could you possibly send this fax for me?
5. Can you let me know your decision as soon as possible?

6. Can you show me a copy of your new brochure?

7. Could you change my flight from Friday to Monday, please?

8. Could I possibly borrow your golf clubs?

PEOPLE AND BUILDINGS

1. headquarters
2. factory/plant
3. board
4. office
5. management/executives
6. warehouse
7. subsidiary
8. importer
9. supplier
10. manufacturer
11. wholesaler
12. retailer
13. consumer
14. staff/employees

4 FACT FINDING

QUESTIONS

1. The hotel information desk

What kind of restaurant is it? *(Caribbean)*

How far is it from here? *(five minutes walk)*

What time would you like to eat? *(8:30 p.m.)*

2. The Air Canada desk

When is the next flight to Vancouver? *(8:20 and 9:55)*

How much does it cost? *($154 one way)*

Which flight would you like, the 8:20 or the 9:55? *(8:20)*

3. A delivery firm

How many boxes do you want to send? *(three large boxes)*

How often do you deliver to Georgetown? *(twice a week)*

How long does it take? *(two days maximum)*

The hotel information desk

A Hello. Can you help me? I want to take some clients out for dinner this evening. Is there a good restaurant near here?

B Yes, there's Chez Jacques. That's excellent.

A Uh-ha. What kind of restaurant is it?

B It does Caribbean food.

A And how far is it from here?

B It's only five minutes walk.

A O.K. Can you reserve a table for me?

B Sure. What time would you like to eat?

A Ah, let's say 8:30. The name is Davis.

The Air Canada desk

A When is the next flight to Vancouver?

B There's one at 8:20 and one at 9:55.

A O.K. How much does it cost?

B $154 one way.

A Can I buy my ticket here?

B Certainly. Which flight would you like?

A The 8:20, please.

A delivery firm

A I'd like to send some boxes of brochures to Georgetown.

B How many boxes do you want to send?

A Three large boxes. How often do you deliver to Georgetown?

B Twice a week, on Tuesdays and Fridays.

A And how long does it take?

B Two days maximum.

WHERE IS IT?

1. bank
2. church
3. art gallery
4. university
5. post office
6. railway station
7. airport
8. police station

LISTEN AND SPEAK

Mark   Hello. I'm Mark Ryan from Business International magazine.

You   *e.g.* How do you? I'm John Smith.

Mark	Could I ask you a few questions about your work?
You	*e.g.* Yes, of course.
Mark	So, what do you do here?
You	*e.g.* I am an account manager.
Mark	I see. So what exactly do you have to do?
You	*e.g.* I manage a sales account for a large customer.
Mark	How many people work in your department?
You	*e.g.* In the sales department? About 30.
Mark	I see. And what do you like about your job?
You	*e.g.* I like negotiating.
Mark	O.K. Thank you very much for your help.
You	*e.g.* Not at all. You're welcome.

5 AN INVOICE FROM A SUPPLIER

DEALING WITH NUMBERS

Listen and repeat.

seven thousand...point three three six...sixty percent...three metres by eight metres by twelve metres...eleven dollars eighty...three-eighths...seven hundred and forty thousand, one hundred and eighty-eight...telephone seven two oh double four one three.

FACT FILE

Spanish Industrial Clothing is based in the industrial north of Spain, 45 kms from Bilbao and 52 kms from San Sebastian. It produces over 70 different products, mainly protective clothing which it supplies to local industries. It has an 18% share of the Spanish market, with a turnover last year of 1.2 billion pesetas. Of this, 150 million came from exports. The company employs 245 people, and over a third of these are women.

Nearest city:	Bilbao (45 kms)
Range of products:	70 different products
Share of home market:	18%
Turnover:	1.2 billion pesetas
Exports:	150 million pesetas
Workforce – total:	245
women:	more than a third (⅓)

ORDERING SUPPLIES

Monique	Hello, Nuria. This is Monique Martin from Duroglas.
Nuria	Hello, Monique. How can I help you?
Monique	I'd like to order some gloves.
Nuria	Fine. One moment, I'll get an order form. O.K. What would you like? The AG 3's?
Monique	We have enough of those, I think, well, perhaps 100 pairs of the AG 3's, size 10.
Nuria	Right. So that's 100 AG 3, size 10.
Monique	Yes. And we also need some AG 7's.
Nuria	Oh, do you know about the new range, the RG 7's?
Monique	RG 7's? No. What are they?
Nuria	Well, they're the same design as the AG 7's but they are much stronger. They're 60% leather.
Monique	Mmm... How much are they?
Nuria	They're 250 pesetas a pair.
Monique	O.K. Well, I need 100 of the size 8's, 200 size 10's and 150 size 12's.
Nuria	I'm sorry. There are no size 12's at the moment. But we have got the AG 7's in size 12.
Monique	I see. O.K.... I'll have 150 of those in that case.
Nuria	O.K. So, that's 100 AG 3 size 10, 150 AG 7 in size 12.
Monique	Right.
Nuria	And for the RG 7's you want 100 size 8 and 200 size 10.
Monique	Yes, that's it.
Nuria	And is there anything else?
Monique	Yes, we need some overalls.
Nuria	Sorry?
Monique	Overalls.
Nuria	Ah, yes, grey or light blue?
Monique	Is there any difference in price?
Nuria	No, they are exactly the same price.
Monique	Right. Can I have 30 medium and 20 large in the grey, and...
Nuria	Just a moment. O.K.
Monique	And 20 small light blue and 10 medium light blue.
Nuria	Did you say 20 medium in the grey?
Monique	No. 30 medium and 20 large.

Nuria	And for the light blue it was 20 small and 10 medium?
Monique	That's right. Can you deliver this week?
Nuria	Yes. No problem.
Monique	Good, O.K. Thanks very much.
Nuria	You're welcome. Thanks for calling. Bye.
Monique	Goodbye.

ORDER FORM

GLOVES

Type	Size	Unit Price	Quantity
	8	175	
AG 3	10	175	100
	12	185	
	8	200	
AG 7	10	200	
	12	200	150
	8	250	100
RG 7	10	250	200
		TOTAL:	

OVERALLS

Colour	Size	Unit Price	Quantity
	Small	2000	
Grey	Medium	2200	30
	Large	2400	20
	Small	2000	20
Light Blue	Medium	2200	10
	Large	2400	
		TOTAL:	

PLACING AN ORDER

2. Telephone the supplier
10. Sign the delivery note
9. Check the goods on arrival
1. Do a stock check
3. Place an order
7. Dispatch the goods
5. Pass the order on to the store manager
8. Deliver the goods
4. Fill out an order form
6. Make up the order

Monique did a stock check. Then she telephoned SIC and she placed an order. Nuria filled out an order form and passed the order on to the store manager. The store manager made up the order and dispatched the goods. SIC delivered the goods. Someone at Duroglas checked the goods on arrival and signed the delivery note.

PRONUNCIATION

Listen and repeat.

wanted...used...ordered...stopped...called...
returned...contacted...asked...decided...arrived...
purchased...prepared.

WHAT WENT WRONG?

1. Perhaps the store manager did not make up the order correctly.
2. Perhaps he did not dispatch the right goods.
3. Perhaps Duroglas did not check the goods carefully.

AN INVOICE FROM A SUPPLIER

Invoice Date	Account Number	Invoice Number (Please quote in all correspondence)			
QUANTITY	DESCRIPTION	List Price	Gross	Discount %	Net
	GLOVES				
100	~~AG3~~ AG7 Size 10	~~175~~ ~~200~~	~~17,500~~ ~~20,000~~	10%	~~15,750~~ ~~18,000~~
150	AG7 Size 12	200	30,000	10%	27,000
100	RG7 Size 8	250	25,000	10%	22,500
~~100~~ 200	RG7 Size 10	250	~~25,000~~ 50,000	10%	~~22,500~~ 45,000
	OVERALLS				
30	Grey: Medium	2200	66,000	10%	59,400
20	Large	2400	48,000	10%	43,200
20	Light blue: Small	2000	40,000	10%	36,000
~~30~~ 10	Medium	2200	~~66,000~~ 22,000	10%	~~59,400~~ 19,800
	Total Goods	Total Discount		Invoice Total	
	Pta ~~320,000~~ 298,500	Pta ~~32,000~~ 29,850		Pta ~~288,000~~ 268,650	

GSA WATER PURIFIERS

1. It is economical.
2. The GSA 500T.
3. b) A jar of marmalade.
4. The number of organisms increases with use.

6 A SITUATION REPORT

MARKET TRENDS

Trends

1. The number of holiday resorts is increasing.
2. Developers are continuing to buy up land for new hotels and apartments.
3. More and more people are trying to find a different kind of holiday.
4. People are travelling longer distances.
5. People, especially in the 40-60 age group, are taking holidays in the low season.
6. Special interest holidays are becoming more popular.

A SITUATION REPORT

Anna	This is Valken Tours. We are sorry that there is no-one in the office to answer your call. Please leave your name and number and we will call you back as soon as possible. Speak after the tone.

Ronald Anna, its Ronnie here. I'm phoning from Cagliari. Look, we have a problem. Did you hear about the fire in the north of the island? Well, no-one was hurt – our people are O.K., but the fire is still spreading. It's very close to two of the farms where people are staying so we're moving them. Two families want to go home. We are putting them on the next plane. But we are not refunding their money. I think their insurance will pay. I'm arranging accommodation in Cagliari for the others. I just hope we can find enough things for them to do here. I'll telephone you again on Monday, but don't take any more bookings for now.

2. He is moving customers to Cagliari.
4. He is putting them on the next plane. He is not refunding their money.

DEALING WITH PROBLEMS (possible answers)

1. We are arranging other transport for the customers.
2. We are looking for another hotel and we are cancelling our contract with the old hotel.
3. We are asking for a new tour leader to come from Holland.
4. We are arranging medical treatment for them and we are taking legal action.

LAWSON EDUCATIONAL BOOKS

1. a) Heinemann
2. a) students and teachers
3. a) to distribute more catalogues to the end-users

ADJECTIVES AND NOUNS

important, useful, brief, recent meeting
nice, good idea
recent, useful report
quick, important, good decision
serious problem
high, good price
heavy loss
recent, important event
nice, heavy, quick meal
tall, nice, kind, young man
fast, modern, large car
modern, large factory
young, nice, large country

7 ENTERTAINING A CLIENT

ENTERTAINING A CLIENT

Waiter

7. Can I take your order now?
15. Is everything O.K.?
9. Would you like a starter?
10. What would you like to drink?
11. Enjoy your meal.
2. Do you have a reservation?

Halima

14. More wine?
17. Please. I'll get this.
16. The bill, please.
3. I recommend the Satay.
1. A table for two please.
12. How is your Satay?

Lisa

13. It's a little too sweet for me.
8. I'll have the Satay.
5. Is it hot?
4. Can you tell me what is in the Satay?
6. Do any vegetables come with it?

LISTEN AND SPEAK

At the airport

Said	Hello. I'm Said Sadr and this is Nasser Ali.
You	*e.g.* Pleased to meet you. I'm John Smith.
Said	Did you have a good flight?
You	*e.g.* Yes, thank you.

At the hotel

Receptionist	Can I take your suitcase for you?
You	*e.g.* It's O.K., thank you. It's not heavy.
Receptionist	Do you have a reservation?
You	*e.g.* Yes. My name is Smith.
Receptionist	Could you spell your name for me, please?
You	*e.g.* Yes. It's S-M-I-T-H.

Buying a film

Sales assistant	Can I help you?
You	*e.g.* Yes. I'd like a film for my camera.
Sales assistant	Would you like 100 ASA or 200 ASA?
You	*e.g.* 100 ASA, please.
Sales assistant	We have a special high quality film, but it's quite expensive.
You	*e.g.* How much is it?

8 AN IMPORTANT MESSAGE

GETTING THROUGH

Caller

I'd like to speak to Mrs Cameron.

Can I speak to someone who deals with...?

Could I have the sales department, please?

No thanks. I'll call back later.

My name is...

I'm inquiring about...

Is that Leo Wan's office?

Switchboard

Who's calling, please?

Hold the line, please.

Sorry. You have the wrong number.

One moment. I'll put you through.

The line's busy. Will you hold?

Knox Oil and Gas. Good afternoon.

Can I tell her who called?

Receiver

Yes, speaking.

Hello. Sales.

Leo Wan here. Can I help you?

Sorry. You have the wrong extension.

1.

B Hello. Argus Engineering.

A Hello. Can I speak to Mr Franks, please?

B Mr Franks? Just a moment...I'm sorry, the line's busy. Will you hold?

A No, that's O.K. I'll call back later.

B Can I tell him who called?

A Yes. My name is Carey: C-A-R-E-Y.

B Right, Mr Carey. I'll tell him you called.

2.

B Gamble and Proud. Good morning.

A Can I have the personnel department, please?

B I'm sorry. Which department?

A The personnel department.

B Just a moment. I'll put you through.

C Personnel.

A Hello. Is Robert Turner there?

C Hold the line. I'll get him for you.

D Hello. Robert Turner here.

3.

B Hello. Japan Airlines.

A Hello. I'm inquiring about flights to Tokyo.

B One moment. I'll put you through to the booking desk.

C International flights. Can I help you?

A Yes. I want to book a flight to Tokyo.

C Certainly, sir. When would you like to travel?

4.

B Hello. Cale and Cale, Solicitors.

A Is that Malcolm Cambell?

B Yes, speaking.

A It's David Lyle here. I need to see you. Can we meet on Friday?

B I'm sorry. I'm busy on Friday. Is Thursday possible for you?

WILL AND 'LL

1. I'll get you a drink.
2. I'll have the steak, in that case.
3. I'll give it to him.
4. I'll take the cheaper one.
5. I'll call them this afternoon.
6. I'll take him one evening.

ON THE PHONE

Example 1.

B Delhi Railway Station.

A I'm inquiring about the times of trains to Calcutta this afternoon.

B One moment, please. When do you want to travel?

A   This afternoon, about five o'clock.

B   There's a train at six-thirty, which arrives in Calcutta at two twenty-five tomorrow morning.

Example 2.

B   Newton, Burns and Kipling.

A   Is that NBK Air Conditioning?

B   Yes, that's right. Can I help you?

A   Yes. Can I have the sales department, please?

B   Hold the line, please. I'll put you through.

A   Thank you.

C   Hello. Sales.

A   Oh, I'd like to order an air conditioning system for an office 30 metres by 50 metres by 3 metres.

C   Sorry? How big is the office?

A   30 by 50 by 3 metres.

Now you try.

(1. and 2. as above)

3.

B   Good evening. Taj Mahal Restaurant.

You   *e.g.* Hello. I'd like to book a table for four for tonight.

B   Yes. What time, please?

You   *e.g.* 8 o'clock.

B   Can I have your name, please?

You   *e.g.* Yes, it is Smith. S-M-I-T-H.

B   O.K. Thank you. Goodbye.

4.

B   Kline Ferguson. Good afternoon and how can I help you?

You   *e.g.* I'd like to speak to Jeff Gomez, please.

B   Who's calling?

You   *e.g.* My name is John Smith.

B   One moment please, caller. I'm sorry. Mr Gomez is not available right now. Can I take a message?

You   *e.g.* No thanks. I'll call back later.

5.

B   Surrey Post.

You   *e.g.* Can I have the advertising department, please.

B   Sure. Hold the line.

C   Hello. Tom Randall speaking.

You   *e.g.* Hello. I'd like to place an advertisement in the business-to-business column.

C   Sorry. You've got the wrong department. You want advertising. I'll put you through.

You   *e.g.* Thank you.

6.

B   Allied Webb Financial Services.

You   *e.g.* I'm inquiring about your U.S. investment fund.

B   Which fund?

You   *e.g.* Your U.S. investment fund.

B   Trying to connect you.

C   Pearl Jackson speaking. How can I help you?

You   *e.g.* Could you send me a brochure about your U.S. investment fund?

C   Could I have your name and address?

AN IMPORTANT MESSAGE (possible answers)

Student A	**Student B**

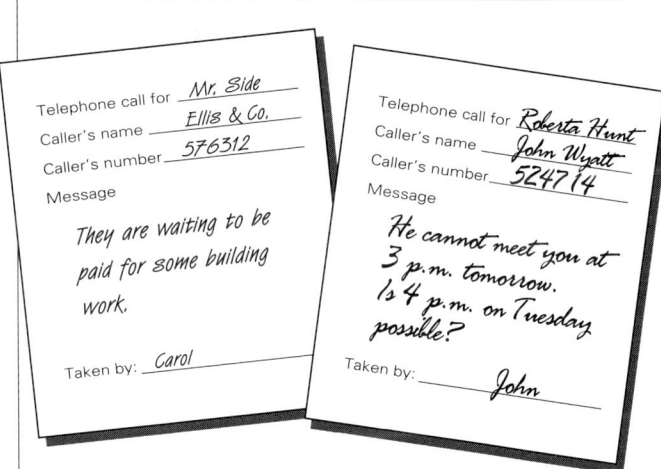

Telephone call for *Mr. Side*
Caller's name *Ellis & Co.*
Caller's number *576312*
Message

They are waiting to be paid for some building work.

Taken by: *Carol*

Telephone call for *Roberta Hunt*
Caller's name *John Wyatt*
Caller's number *524714*
Message

He cannot meet you at 3 p.m. tomorrow. Is 4 p.m. on Tuesday possible?

Taken by: *John*

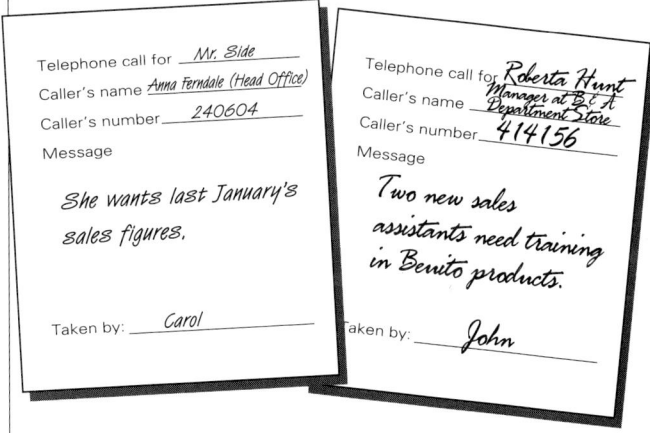

Telephone call for *Mr. Side*
Caller's name *Anna Ferndale (Head Office)*
Caller's number *240604*
Message

She wants last January's sales figures.

Taken by: *Carol*

Telephone call for *Roberta Hunt*
Caller's name *Manager at B&A Department Store*
Caller's number *414156*
Message

Two new sales assistants need training in Benito products.

Taken by: *John*

TELECOMMUNICATIONS

1. screen
2. keyboard
3. public telephone
4. portable handset

MONEY

1. I have got $6000. I can either _invest_ it on the stock market or I can _save_ it for my next holiday.
2. He never has any money because he _spends_ more than he _earns_.
3. The company plans to increase the _wages_ of factory personnel by 10%. Directors' _salaries_ will only go up by 4%.
4. Please pay your hotel and restaurant _bill (check)_ now and you can send us an _invoice_ for all your expenses at the end of the trip.
5. The car _cost_ £5000 in 1989 but now it _is worth_ only £600.
6. I must _pay back_ the $1200 that I _owe_ to the bank. I can't _afford_ the interest.
7. Don't _waste_ your money on a train ticket. You can _save_ £6, if you go by bus.
8. There is no extra _charge_ for delivery; it's included in the _price_.

9 A LOOK AT THE FIGURES

DESCRIBING PERFORMANCE

1. Output went up/rose/increased
2. Inflation fell/went down/dropped
3. Exports were/stood at/
4. Unemployment stayed the same/remained at last month's level

DESCRIBING A GRAPH

1. _In_ January 1986, sales stood at £900 million.
2. _Over_ the next 12 months they rose _slightly_.
3. But _at the beginning of_ 1987 they dropped _sharply_ to £700 million.
4. They remained at this level _until_ the end of 1987.
5. _Between_ 1988 _and_ 1990 they increased _rapidly_ and reached £1,250 million.
6. In 1990 they continued to rise, but more _slowly_ and _at the end of_ 1990 sales were £1,380 million.

A SALES REPORT

1. Why were sales slow in Japan at the beginning of the year?
2. When did the situation improve?
3. Why didn't sales in the U.S. increase?
4. What was the best selling children's antibiotic in 1989?
5. Why did they launch Junior Trioxil in 1990?

A LOOK AT THE FIGURES

Kristina In 1987, the Healthcare Exhibition moved from Geneva to a bigger exhibition centre in Zurich, so many more exhibitors were able to attend. But the first exhibition in Zurich was badly organized and, because of this, the number of exhibitors dropped in 1988. The organizers wanted to make sure that this did not happen again, so, in 1989, they reduced the cost of a stand and sent letters to hundreds of companies, advertising the exhibition. Over the next two years the number of exhibitors rose sharply. In 1991 the organizers opened the exhibition to non-European companies and in that year 118 companies attended.

Over 85,000 visitors came to the Healthcare Exhibition on the first day. This was due to a good publicity campaign and because May the 1st is a public holiday in Switzerland. However, on the second day the weather was bad and many people stayed at home. On Wednesday, another important exhibition – Salvacon 93 – opened in Zurich, and the number of visitors fell again. Because of this, the organizers decided to make entrance to the exhibition free from Thursday. Their idea worked and 300,000 people visited the exhibition over the last four days.

Number of exhibitors

A. exhibition moves to bigger centre
B. bad organization
C. publicity campaign and cost of a stand goes down
D. exhibition opened to non-European companies

Number of visitors

A. publicity campaign and public holiday
B. bad weather
C. other exhibition opens
D. entrance free

SALES AND MARKETING

a sales target

a special offer

a competitive market

market research

a product range

an advertising campaign

a major competitor

an up-market image

a retail outlet

a brand name

10 SAYING THE RIGHT THING

SHORT ANSWERS

1. Yes, I am.
2. No, it isn't.
3. No, I don't.
4. Yes, he does.
5. Yes, it was.
6. No, I didn't.
7. Yes, he did./No, he didn't.
8. Yes, you are./No, you aren't.
9. Yes, it does./No, it doesn't.
10. Yes, they were./No, they weren't.
11. Yes, it is./No, it isn't.
12. Yes, they are./No, they aren't.

SAYING THE RIGHT THING (possible answers)

He says	You say
Excuse me. Can I sit here?	Yes. Please do.
It's a beautiful evening, isn't it?	Yes, it is.
I see you are reading a German book. Are you from Germany?	No, actually. I'm French.
Really? Where are you from exactly?	Marseilles.
I know it well. I was there only last year.	Really? Did you like it?
Oh, it was fantastic. I was on holiday with my family for two weeks. We wanted to stay longer, but my wife was ill and we had to come back.	Oh. I'm sorry to hear that.

Oh, she's fine now. Are you on holiday here?	No, actually. I'm on business.
And you're staying at this hotel?	Yes, that's right.
Can I get you a drink? I'm going to have one.	That's very kind of you.
Sorry, I couldn't get a drink. The bar's closed.	Never mind.
Would you like coffee instead?	No, thanks.
So...is it your first visit here?	Yes, it is.
Will there be any more in the future?	I hope so.
Well, I hope so. Prague is a beautiful city.	Yes, it is.
Well...will you excuse me? I need to make a phone call. Do you know if there is a public telephone in the hotel?	I'm not sure.
O.K. See you again, perhaps.	Yes. I hope so.

LISTEN AND SPEAK

At passport control

Immigration Officer	What's your job?
You	*e.g.* I'm sales director for Ellen International.
Immigration Officer	Is it your first time in the States?
You	*e.g.* Yes, it is.
Immigration Officer	And why are you here?
You	*e.g.* I'm here on business.

Telephoning Mike Bukowski

Switchboard	Hello. S.B. and K. Can I help you?
You	*e.g.* Yes. Can I speak to Mr Bukowski, please?
Mike	Mike Bukowski here. So, you've arrived safely. Which hotel are you staying at?
You	*e.g.* I'm at the Ritz.
Mike	Would you like to have lunch with me?
You	*e.g.* Yes, thank you.
Mike	O.K. I'll be there in 10 minutes. Where will you wait?
You	*e.g.* I'll be at reception.

At lunch

Mike	More wine?
You	*e.g.* Thanks, just a little.
Mike	So, sales were bad last month. Why was that?
You	*e.g.* Well, I think it was due to the competition.
Mike	Do you think next month will be better?
You	*e.g.* I hope so. We are launching a new product in June.

11 A MANUFACTURING PROCESS

INSTRUCTIONS

1. First insert the card. Then key in your personal number and wait for the machine to check it. Next, select the amount of money and press **enter**. Finally, remove the card, and don't forget to take your cash.

2. First of all, place the jack under the car. Then loosen the wheel nuts. After that, raise the car until the wheel is off the ground and remove the wheel nuts and the wheel. Put the new wheel on and replace the wheel nuts. Then lower the car. Make sure you tighten the wheel nuts.

3. First of all, make sure you keep your receipts. Then fill in the claim form at the end of the month and ask the head of your department to sign the form. Finally give the form and the receipts to the accounts department.

ACTIVE AND PASSIVE

1. At reception: Visitors are asked to sign the visitors' book.
2. In a car park: This parking space is reserved for visitors.
3. On the box: Batteries are not supplied with this unit.
4. On the guarantee: Every toy is checked before it leaves the factory.
5. By the cash till in a shop: Cheques are only accepted with identification.

6. New products *are developed* *by* the R and D Department.
7. The tests *are done* *in* a laboratory.
8. Most of our goods *are delivered* *by* truck.
9. 70% of our cars *are assembled* *by* robot.
10. The oil *is stored* *in* large tanks.

A MANUFACTURING PROCESS

Britt Our production department is quite small. Because the process is fully automated, we employ only 12 people in the match factory. We produce about 6 billion matches a year – that's 800 boxes every minute – and the whole process takes about one and a half hours.

First the logs are cut into thin sticks, about 3 centimetres long. These sticks are then put into a bath of ammonium phosphate. Ammonium phosphate is a retarding agent which makes sure that the match stops burning when you blow it out...like this.

Next the match sticks are cleaned and then they are transferred to a slow-moving conveyor belt. As they travel along the conveyor belt, one end of the match stick is coated with hot paraffin wax and an explosive chemical is added. This is the match head. The paraffin wax helps the match burn.

The matches are now dried and when they reach the end of the conveyor belt they are punched into boxes, about 50 at a time.

Finally the box covers are pushed onto the boxes and the matches are ready for dispatch.

1.	cut	6.	add
2.	put into	7.	dry
3.	clean	8.	punch
4.	transfer	9.	push
5.	coat		

THE KAWASAKI PRODUCTION SYSTEM

It uses simple ideas and cheap solutions to reduce waste and continuously improve the process.

12 A NEW PRODUCT

DESCRIBING PRODUCTS

Calculator: It works like an ordinary calculator, but it doesn't need a battery. The photo cells absorb light and this energy is used to power the calculator. It cannot be used in the dark.

Executive Toy: When you lift the right-hand ball out to the right and then release it, it swings back and strikes the ball next to it. The energy is transferred through the other balls to the one at the opposite end, which is pushed up and out. If you lift two balls and release them together, two balls move at the other end.

Smoke Filter: The motor is powered by electricity. When it is switched on, it turns the fan. The fan sucks air into the machine and down through the filter where it is cleaned.

THE BEST PRODUCT

Zenon makes the quietest photocopiers on the market.

Alpha makes the most accurate watches on the market.

Matteson makes the strongest glue on the market.

Firesteam makes the safest tyres on the market.

Evac makes the most powerful vacuum cleaners on the market.

Comfit makes the most comfortable mattresses on the market.

PRODUCT FEATURES

Company Approach

1. To be flexible.
2. To be fast.
3. To invest in R & D.
4. To care about people and the environment.

Product Features

1. A range of colours, shapes and sizes.
2. Custom-built products supplied in any quantity.
3. A range of caps.
4. 60% biodegradable.
5. Childproof and safe caps.

A NEW PRODUCT

Account Executive Well, thank you for asking me here today. I'd like to talk to you about the packaging for Jocasta shampoo and show you our new design for the bottle.

As you know, the Jocasta shampoo bottle has an unusual shape, different from other shampoo bottles on the market. We want to keep this shape because we believe the customer can easily recognize it. In other words, it's an important part of Jocasta's image.

So what is new about our design? Today's consumers want two things: first, they want a bottle that is easy to use; second, they want to look after their environment. Our design provides both these features. First, the cap. It's clean, simple and easy to use. The shampoo comes out of a hole in the cap which can be opened simply by pressing down one side of it. No drips, no mess, no need to wash the bottle.

What happens when the bottle is finished? The old bottle was thrown away. Expensive and bad for the environment. With our new bottle you just buy a refill. The refill comes in a small biodegradable packet with a tube at the top. Remove the end of the tube, pour the shampoo into the old bottle and replace the cap.

Audience O.K., but what about the cost?

Account Executive The refill is about 40% cheaper to produce than the bottle. So the customer can help the environment and, at the same time, actually save money. O.K. I think that's all. If there are any other questions, I'll be happy to...

1. He is describing B.
2. The reasons for this design are that:
   - it keeps the recognized shape.
   - the cap is easy to use and clean.
   - the bottle can be used again so it is better for the environment and cheaper.

AN ADVERTISING BRIEF

The features used in the advertisement are:
- efficiency
- competitive prices
- they are the second largest company in the market

VERBS AND NOUNS

make, take notes (on it)

have, make an appointment (with him)

do, make a deal (with her)

do research (into it)

make a profit/loss (on it)

make a suggestion

have a meeting/discussion (about it)

give, have a reason (for it)

do something (about it)

13 A FIVE-YEAR PLAN

EXPRESSING PURPOSE (possible answers)

1. She telephoned the travel agent to book a flight.
2. She went to the market to buy some vegetables.
3. She stopped at the petrol (gas) station to get some petrol (gas).
4. She went to the library to borrow a book.
5. She bought some glue to repair a chair.
6. She visited the museum to see a new exhibition.

PLANS AND INTENTIONS

He is going to visit/is thinking of visiting the suppliers to negotiate new contracts.

He is going to hold/is thinking of holding daily meetings with the production foreman to discuss production problems.

He is going to hold/is thinking of holding weekly meetings with union representatives to improve relations between workers and management.

He is going to do/is thinking of doing a work study to improve efficiency.

He is going to close/is thinking of closing the factory for three days to install new machinery.

GOVERNMENT PLANS

close down an old hospital

restrict foreign investment

nationalize large industries

abolish a youth training programme

reduce public spending

dismiss/fire the Minister for Transport

MAKING PREDICTIONS

If the Conservatives win, they will (probably) reduce taxes.

If the Conservatives win, they will (probably) encourage exports.

If the Conservatives win, they will (probably) increase military spending.

If the Conservatives win, they will (probably) build more private schools.

If the Conservatives win, they will (probably) encourage small businesses.

If the Conservatives win, they will (probably) privatize public transport.

If the Socialists win, they will (probably) increase taxes.

If the Socialists win, they will (probably) restrict imports.

If the Socialists win, they will (probably) reduce military spending.

If the Socialists win, they will (probably) abolish private education.

If the Socialists win, they will (probably) nationalize large industries.

If the Socialists win, they will (probably) improve public transport.

A FIVE-YEAR PLAN

Mr Harada And so, as you can see, last year was a difficult but interesting year for our company. Now, what about the future?

Times are changing in the car industry and over the next five years we will have to make some difficult decisions. But, Toida is an experienced company and if we make changes now, we will improve our strong position in the market.

At the end of next year we are going to close down our plant in Tokyo and stop production of the 620, our luxury saloon car. With the money from this sale we are going to do two things. Firstly, we are going to produce more small motorcycles to meet the increasing demand. Secondly, we are going to expand our research centre in Nagoya. This will be a centre for the development of a new range of cars for the 21st century – cars which don't use gasoline. Our first gasoline-free car will be launched next year. I cannot tell you more now, but I can tell you that it is not an electric car.

The Insurance Services division is doing very well and over the next two years we are going to open twelve new offices in Japan. To manage this fast growing business, I am going to appoint Mr Naitoh as vice-president of marketing. Our aim is to have a 20% share of the Japanese market in the next five years.

Many of you want to know when I am going to retire. The answer is simple. I am thinking of retiring...when I am too old for the job.

Mr Harada is going to close down the plant in Tokyo.

Mr Harada is going to increase production of motorcycles to meet demand.

Mr Harada is going to expand the research centre in Nagoya to develop a new range of gasoline-free cars.

Mr Harada is going to open 12 new insurance offices and appoint Mr Naitoh as vice-president of marketing to get a 20% share of the Japanese insurance market.

Mr Harada is not going to retire yet.

PROFIT AND LOSS ACCOUNT (possible answers)

Labour costs were higher because of a wage increase for factory workers.

Salaries were higher because the company employed a new marketing assistant.

Building maintenance was higher because of new safety laws.

Finance costs (loans) were higher because interest rates increased by 1.5%.

New building costs: a second car park was built.

FINANCE

1. The marketing department wants to increase its _budget_ by 15% next year.
2. We have a lot of _overheads_ – heating, lighting, office supplies, rent etc.
3. The _forecast_ for next year is very good.
4. Salaries are 38% of our total _costs_ .
5. We have a lot of _capital_ invested in these machines.

14 MAKING AN ARRANGEMENT

ARRANGING A MEETING

1.

Wayne Hello, Judy. It's Wayne here. Look, I'd like to meet you to discuss your report.

Judy O.K. Where shall we meet?

Wayne How about the Carlton? We could have lunch first.

Judy That sounds great.

Wayne Does Thursday suit you?

Judy Yes. That's fine. What time?

Wayne I'll meet you in the bar at one o'clock.

Judy Good. See you then.

2.

Janine Hello, it's Janine here. I'm calling about our Wednesday appointment. I'm afraid I can't make it that day. Can we change it to another day?

Pardoe Yes, that's O.K. When?

Janine What about Thursday morning?

Pardoe Thursday is fine.

Janine Good. Shall we say 10:30?

Pardoe 10:30? 11:30 suits me better.

Janine O.K. I'll see you on Thursday at 11:30.

Pardoe Fine. Bye.

A VISIT FROM A VIP

He is arriving at the airport at 3 p.m. on Tuesday. JB is meeting him there. Then he is having drinks with the management at 4:00. I am taking him to his hotel at about 5:30 and in the evening he is going to the opera with FW. On Wednesday he is having a meeting with FW and then at 10:00 he is opening the new research centre. He is giving a press conference at 11:00 and after that he is having lunch with some local VIP's. In the afternoon we are taking him on a boat trip around Sydney Harbour. He is flying home at 7:40 in the evening.

LISTEN AND SPEAK
Mr Dillinger's arrival

Mr Dillinger	How do you do? I'm Mr Dillinger.
You	*e.g.* How do you do? I'm Julian Barnes.
Mr Dillinger	And you're from personnel, aren't you?
You	*e.g.* Yes, that's right.
Mr Dillinger	O.K. Where are we going this afternoon?
You	*e.g.* We are going to look around the new research centre.

At the research centre

Mr Dillinger	So how is this new research centre different from the old one?
You	*e.g.* Well, it's much bigger and the equipment is more modern.
Mr Dillinger	How much did it cost to build?
You	*e.g.* Around $2 million.
Mr Dillinger	And how many engineers will work here?
You	*e.g.* 8 engineers and about 25 technicians.
Mr Dillinger	What happens in this section?
You	*e.g.* This is where tests are done on new equipment.
Mr Dillinger	Well, thanks for showing me around.
You	*e.g.* It was a pleasure.

15 A PROGRESS REPORT

HISTORICAL EVENTS

1. The Panama Canal _was opened_ in _1914_.
2. Romeo and Juliet _was written_ in _1597_.
3. The first communications satellite _was launched_ in _1957_.
4. The Great Wall of China _was built_ in _210 BC_.
5. Rolls Royce _was founded_ in _1906_.
6. East and West Germany _were unified_ in _1990_.
7. Television _was invented_ in _1926_.

COMPANY HISTORY

Metropolitan Bank was founded over 80 years ago in Dijon by Georges Marquet. It expanded rapidly during the 1920's and branches were opened in Paris, Marseilles, and Lyon. In 1936 Marquet was killed in a plane crash and the company was taken over by Marquet's two sons, Pierre and Hubert. After the war it merged with Banque Liègeois de Commerce. The following year international branches were opened in London, Milan, Geneva, and Frankfurt. In July 1980 the directors of BLC were fired in a scandal. Last year Christophe Marquet was appointed president.

AN UPDATE

Christophe	So, Margit, you're working on promoting customer services.
Margit	Yes, that's right. We are promoting our free information and advice services - advice on pensions, investment, insurances, and so on. We have provided these services for some years, but many of our customers don't know about them.
Christophe	I see. So how have you marketed them?
Margit	Well, firstly, we have provided more literature about them. We have put information leaflets in all local and main branches and we have sent many out to our customers with their monthly statements. We have also run a TV advertising campaign, showing that we give free and impartial advice. In our main branches we have opened Business Advice Centres to help small businesses. For each centre we have appointed a chief advisor, and these men and women have been on a one-week training course, organized by headquarters.
Christophe	And the cost of all this?
Margit	So far we have spent $3 million. But we are already seeing results. We have had 1400 new customers since October and many more of our existing customers have used the services.

1. They have put them in all local and main branches. They have sent them to customers.
2. They have run a TV campaign.
3. They have opened Advice Centres in main branches. They have appointed chief advisors for these centres.
4. They have had 1400 new customers since October.
5. They have spent $3 million.

A PROGRESS REPORT

PROJECT: Beazely Housing
DATE STARTED: 3 years ago
AIMS: To provide better housing and local facilities
ACTION TAKEN: 150 houses built, extensive road building programme
MONEY SPENT: £64 million
POSITIVE RESULTS: New businesses moved to the area
NEGATIVE RESULTS: The new houses were too expensive for local people and outsiders have moved into them
FUTURE PLANS: To build more houses and a business park
MONEY NEEDED: £28 million

PROJECT: Anglia Fruit Co-operative (AFC)
DATE STARTED: 2 years ago
AIMS: To compete with larger fruit producers
ACTION TAKEN: Packing plant and two new warehouses built, money invested in transport to distribute the goods
MONEY SPENT: £7 million
POSITIVE RESULTS: Increased production, deals with two major supermarket chains
NEGATIVE RESULTS: Not all farmers joined, exports have not increased
FUTURE PLANS: To market products in Europe
MONEY NEEDED: £6 million

PERSONAL CHARACTERISTICS (suggested answers)

Salesman	General Manager
persuasive	decisive
ambitious	persuasive
hard-working	thorough
tough	tough
sociable	calm
reliable	hard-working
	honest

Development Engineer	Personnel Manager
thorough	understanding
hard-working	sociable
patient	patient
creative	open-minded
open-minded	calm
	cautious

Listen and repeat.

persuasive...patient...open-minded...thorough...
ambitious... understanding...reliable...sociable...
cautious.

16 A PERSONNEL PROBLEM

SHOULD AND SHOULDN'T

1. We should accept their offer.
2. We should transfer her.
3. We shouldn't take his advice.
4. We should cancel the course.
5. We should arrange a meeting with them.
6. We should not allow smoking in the plant.
7. We should choose the best solution.

GIVING OPINIONS

I don't agree. I think it is much more important to teach them to be independent and to think for themselves.

On the whole, in companies where there is good communication between the management and the workers there are no industrial problems.

Yes, but it depends on the sport. In mountain climbing, for example, there's often a great deal of danger. But I certainly don't think we should stop people from doing it.

I agree. If you can explain to them what they have done wrong, that's fine. But sometimes children, especially young children, cannot understand what the problem is. Then there is no other way.

That's not the point. We want the best person for the job - male or female - it makes no difference.

Subject	Opinion
Strikes	Agrees.
Dangerous sports	It depends on the sport.
Smacking children	It's sometimes necessary.
Employment of women	It depends on the woman.

PERSONNEL MANAGEMENT

to give advice on pensions:	E
to help with personal problems:	B
to encourage health and safety:	F, G
to recruit new staff:	C
to discuss salaries:	D
to train staff:	A

A PUZZLE

Mr Smart should take a stone out of the bag and quickly drop it on the ground with the other stones. Then he should say, "Never mind. If we look at the one still in the bag, we will know what colour the other one was."

17 A JOINT VENTURE

DISCUSSING OPTIONS

A So, as you can see from our market research, the problem is not the product itself, but its image. Today's consumers want a healthy drink and they don't realize that Rico **is** a healthy drink. So we propose giving Rico a new, greener image. Of course, if we do this, we will have to design new packaging, and run a sales campaign.

B But that would be very costly. And are you sure that just changing the packaging will really help our image? I think it would be better if we gave it a new name.

C So, there are two options open to us: one, we stay here on this site and expand and modernize our factory; or two, we move to the new – larger – site outside Düsseldorf. Personally, I feel we should stay. Düsseldorf is too far from our main suppliers. Moving would increase our production costs by 10%.

D I agree. Also if we move, we will lose valuable production time, and many of our skilled workers will stay here and look for other work in the area.

The first speakers are talking about the image of their drink, Rico. The second speakers are talking about moving their factory to another site.

The first speakers can either change the packaging, or they can give it a new name. The second speakers can either modernize and expand their existing plant, or they can move to a new site.

1. If more people _thought_ Rico was a healthy product, its sales _would_ _increase_ .
2. But if the company _changes_ the packaging, _will_ it really _help_ Rico's image?
3. Perhaps they _will_ only _change_ the image, if they _give_ Rico a new name.
4. If they _stay_ where they are now, they _will_ _have_ to expand and modernize their factory.
5. The Düsseldorf site _would_ _be_ a better option, if it _were_ nearer to the company's main suppliers.
6. There is a danger that if they _move_ to Düsseldorf, they _will_ _lose_ many of their skilled workers.

THE HI-FI MARKET

1. The average user and the specialist user.
2. The average user buys a complete system; the specialist buys different components, or a package of individual units.

AN AGENCY AGREEMENT

1. False (from 21 June 1991 to 20 June 1993).
2. True (sole representative).
3. True (all orders shall be transmitted to the Principal).
4. False (they can, but only with the Principal's permission).

18 TAKING PART IN A MEETING

PRESENTING AN ARGUMENT

Purchasing Manager It will not be easy to find the right supplier, _that is to say_ a company which can supply good quality clocks at a good price. Fantoni's designs are not very modern, but _on the other hand_ their clocks are cheap and reliable.

Sales Manager What do you mean? Last month we had to send 50 back.

Purchasing Manager _The point is_ we know them and they know us. If we use another company, Sikur, _for example_ , we have to start from the beginning again and _anyway_ Fantoni is trying to improve reliability.

19 CORRESPONDENCE

REASONS FOR WRITING

I am writing to apologize for the delay.

I am writing in answer to your letter of 25 June.

I am writing to thank you for sending me the books.

I am writing to inquire about your English courses.

I am writing to inform you that I will not be able to come to your reception.

I am writing regarding the order we received.

TYPES OF LETTER

1. An inquiry
2. A covering letter
3. An invitation
4. A thank-you letter

COMMON EXPRESSIONS

concerning	give my regards to	we enclose
with regard to	best wishes to	please find
regarding		enclosed
		attached is

CORRESPONDENCE

STUDENT A

Dear Sirs,

I am writing concerning my reservation. I received confirmation of this yesterday but there were some mistakes. Firstly, it should be 3-5 June and not May. Secondly, I only wanted a single room, and not a suite.

Please could you send me confirmation of the correct details as soon as possible.

I look forward to hearing from you.

Yours faithfully,

Dear Mr/Ms...

I'm writing in answer to your letter of 3rd July. With regard to the promotional video for your company, I'm afraid that I am not able to help you at the moment as I am very busy with other work.

I wish you success with your project. Please contact me if I can help you in the future.

Yours sincerely,

STUDENT B

Dear Mr Sherman,

I am writing to ask for your help in making a promotional video for our company. I was given your name by a friend who recommended your services.

Perhaps we could meet for lunch to discuss this.

I look forward to hearing from you.

Yours sincerely,

Dear Mr/Ms...
Thank you for your letter regarding your hotel booking for June. We apologize for the mistake in the booking and confirm that we have reserved a single room for you from June 3-5 at a cost of $85 a night.
Yours sincerely,

20 REVIEW

SURVIVAL ENGLISH (possible answers)

1. How far is it (from here) to Bond Street?
2. I am here for a meeting with John Sykes. He's expecting me.
3. How much does/will it cost to Bond Street?/How much is it to Bond Street?
4. Hello. Don't I know you?/Haven't we met before?
5. Is there somewhere I can get something to eat?
6. Yes, that's fine./No I'm sorry. I'm in a hurry.
7. Have you got X magazine?
8. Are you going to/Will you be at the Tokyo conference next year?
9. Shall we have lunch together?/Would you like to have lunch?/How about lunch?
10. I'd like a cheese sandwich, please./I'll have a cheese sandwich.
11. That's all right.
12. £10.50? At the station you said £3.00.
13. I'm afraid I'm going to be late. Please start the meeting without me.
14. Fine, thank you. And you?/ Fine. Good to see you too.
15. I'm afraid I couldn't get your magazine./I'm sorry. They didn't have your magazine at the shop.

VOCABULARY REVIEW

1. to disagree
   to forget
   to fall
   to lose
   to buy
   thin
   slow
   dangerous
   tiny
   wrong, left

2. research and development
   supply and demand
   import and export
   health and safety
   profit and loss

3. client, purchaser
   plant
   brochure, price list
   discount
   steel, copper
   goods, services
   invoice

4.

meetings	production	marketing
discuss	machine	promotion
comment	component	launch
recommend	assemble	brand
chairperson	lever	image
agenda	operate	advertisement
attend	process	campaign

finance	communications	personnel
budget	letter	pension
turnover	memo	retire
profit	report	lay off
overheads	fax	training
costs	inquiry	staff
loss	message	recruit

TAPESCRIPTS AND KEY

KEY TO DIAGNOSTIC GRAMMAR TEST

Check your answers. If you have answered a question wrongly (or correctly, but don't know why), refer to the Grammar Points shown.

	Answer	Grammar Point	Page
1.	makes/produces/sells	Present Simple	82
2.	is living/working/etc.	Present Continuous	84
3.	How much?/What	**how much? and how many?**	102
4.	some	**some and any**	101
5.	There are	**There is/There are**	83
6.	Would	**would like and want**	106
7.	Have you met	Present Perfect	89
8.	am having	Present Continuous (Future)	87
9.	was built	Passive	92
10.	leaves	1st Conditional	90
11.	to buy/to get/for	Infinitive of Purpose	106
12.	you to/him to/etc.	**would like and want**	106
13.	minutes ago/years ago/etc.	Past Simple	88
14.	well	Adverbs	96
15.	bigger/more expensive/etc.	Comparison of Adjectives	99
16.	often does	Present Simple	82
17.	shall/can/could	**shall/can and could**	94
18.	Can you/Could you	**can and could**	94
19.	had/knew	2nd Conditional	91
20.	After/Before	No Article	104
21.	Did you/she/etc.	Past Simple	88
22.	should	**should and ought to**	95
23.	I'll/We'll	**will**	86
24.	it was	Pronouns	105
25.	didn't	**must, have to, and need to**	94
26.	has worked	Present Perfect	89
27.	the longest	Comparison of Adjectives	99
28.	are going/planning	**going to**	86
29.	Is there	**There is/There are**	83
30.	will	1st Conditional	90

KEY TO GRAMMAR EXERCISES

EXERCISE 1

1. am trying
2. does not come
3. reads
4. am reading
5. do you write
6. do not serve
7. is not working
8. is improving

EXERCISE 2

1. have not published
2. went
3. have sold
4. have worked
5. has not left
6. happened

EXERCISE 3

1. has been stolen
2. was fired
3. will be told
4. should be faxed
5. are sold
6. is going to be closed down

EXERCISE 4

1. a)
2. c)
3. b)
4. a)
5. c)
6. a)
7. b)
8. a)

EXERCISE 5

1. Wrong (her real name)
2. Wrong (always lived)
3. Right
4. Right
5. Right
6. Wrong (good)
7. Right
8. Wrong (a black and gold uniform)

EXERCISE 6

1. a)
2. c)
3. b)
4. b)
5. c)
6. a)
7. a)
8. b)

EXERCISE 7

1. the
2. the, —
3. a
4. The
5. (some), —
6. a, the

EXERCISE 8

When John asked me to go on holiday with _him_ to Norway, I thought _it_ was a good idea and _I_ agreed. It was only when _we_ arrived in Nordkapp three weeks later with _our_ tent that I realized _my_ mistake. _It_ was −18° C and the days were only four hours long. We had warm clothes with _us_ , but no proper sleeping bags. John's sleeping bag was quite new, but _mine_ was 20 years old.

IRREGULAR VERBS

Present	Past	Past Participle
am-are-is	was-were	been
become	became	become
begin	began	begun
break	broke	broken
bring	brought	brought
build	built	built
buy	bought	bought
catch	caught	caught
choose	chose	chosen
come	came	come
cost	cost	cost
deal	dealt	dealt
do	did	done
eat	ate	eaten
fall	fell	fallen
feel	felt	felt
find	found	found
fly	flew	flown
forget	forgot	forgotten
get	got	got (gotten in U.S. English)
give	gave	given
go	went	gone
grow	grew	grown
have/has	had	had
hear	heard	heard
hit	hit	hit
hold	held	held
keep	kept	kept
know	knew	known
learn	learnt/learned	learnt/learned
leave	left	left
lend	lent	lent
let	let	let
lose	lost	lost
make	made	made
mean	meant	meant
meet	met	met
pay	paid	paid
put	put	put
read	read	read
rise	rose	risen
run	ran	run

Present	Past	Past Participle
say	said	said
see	saw	saw
sell	sold	sold
send	sent	sent
set	set	set
show	showed	shown/showed
sit	sat	sat
speak	spoke	spoken
spell	spelt/spelled	spelt/spelled
spend	spent	spent
stand	stood	stood
steal	stole	stolen
take	took	taken
teach	taught	taught
tell	told	told
think	thought	thought
throw	threw	thrown
understand	understood	understood
wear	wore	worn
win	won	won
write	wrote	written

PRONUNCIATION CHART

VOWELS		CONSONANTS	
/ɪ/	as in sit	/p/	as in put
/iː/	as in see	/b/	as in but
/ʊ/	as in book	/t/	as in ten
/uː/	as in you	/d/	as in dog
/e/	as in red	/f/	as in fat
/ə/	as in camera	/v/	as in very
/ɜː/	as in girl		
		/m/	as in man
/ʌ/	as in but	/n/	as in not
/æ/	as in man	/ŋ/	as in sing
/ɒ/	as in hot		
		/s/	as in sun/thinks
/ɔː/	as in door	/z/	as in zoo/lose
/ɑː/	as in car		
		/k/	as in come
/eɪ/	as in day	/g/	as in go
/aɪ/	as in why		
		/θ/	as in think
/ɔɪ/	as in boy	/ð/	as in this
/ɪə/	as in dear		
		/ʃ/	as in shoe
/ʊə/	as in sure	/tʃ/	as in change
/eə/	as in chair		
		/dʒ/	as in judge
/əʊ/	as in go	/ʒ/	as in television
/aʊ/	as in how		
		/l/	as in look
		/r/	as in right
		/w/	as in water
		/h/	as in hot
		/j/	as in young

WORD LIST

(adj) = adjective   to = verb

(prep) = preposition   (adv) = adverb

a(n) = countable noun   ( ) = uncountable noun

(n.pl.) = plural noun

Under **meaning** write a sentence using this word OR write another word which has the same meaning OR write a translation.

NOTE: Many English words have more than one form and more than one meaning.

e.g.   to **credit** some money to an account (verb)

       a **credit** of £10 was paid to your account (countable noun)

       a **credit** balance (adjective)

       to be refused **credit** (uncountable noun)

Check your dictionary for additional forms and meanings to those listed here.

Word		**Meaning**
to	abolish /əbɒlɪʃ/	
(adv)	abroad /əbrɔːd/	
to	accept /əksept/	
( )	accommodation /əkɒmədeɪʃən/	
an	account /əkaʊnt/	
an	accountant	
(adj)	accurate /ækjərət/	
(adv)	actually /æktʃʊəlɪ/	
to	add /æd/	
( )	administration /ədmɪnɪstreɪʃən/	
to	advertise /ædvətaɪz/	
an	advertisement /ədvɜːtɪsmənt/	
( )	advice /ədvaɪs/	
to	advise /ədvaɪz/	
to	afford /əfɔːd/	
(adj)	afraid /əfreɪd/	
an	agency /eɪdʒənsɪ/	
an	agent	
to	agree /əgriː/	
an	aim /eɪm/	
to	allow /əlaʊ/	
an	amount /əmaʊnt/	
(adj)	annual /ænjʊəl/	
an	answer /ɑːnsə/	
to	apologize /əpɒlədʒaɪz/	
to	apply for /əplaɪ/	

Word		**Meaning**
to	appoint /əpɔɪnt/	
to	approach /əprəʊtʃ/	
(adv)	approximately /əprɒksɪmətlɪ/	
an	area /eərɪə/	
to	arrange /əreɪndʒ/	
to	ask for /ɑːsk/	
an	assistant /əsɪstənt/	
to	attend /ətend/	
(adj)	attractive /ətræktɪv/	
an	audit /ɔːdɪt/	
(adj)	automatic /ɔːtəmætɪk/	
(adj)	available /əveɪləbəl/	
an	average /ævərɪdʒ/	
a	base /beɪs/	
(adj)	based in /beɪst/	
(adj)	based on	
a	batch /bætʃ/	
a	battery /bætərɪ/	
a	beginning /bɪgɪnɪŋ/	
(prep)	behind /bɪhaɪnd/	
to	believe /bɪliːv/	
a	benefit /benɪfɪt/	
(prep)	between /bɪtwiːn/	
a	bill (check) /bɪl/	
a	board /bɔːd/	
a	bonus /bəʊnəs/	
to	book /bʊk/	
to	borrow /bɒrəʊ/	
a	branch /brɑːntʃ/	
a	brand /brænd/	
to	break down /breɪk/	
(adj)	brief /briːf/	
a	brochure /brəʊʃə/	
a	budget /bʌdʒɪt/	
to	build /bɪld/	
( )	bulk /bʌlk/	
( )	business /bɪznɪs/	
(adj)	busy /bɪzɪ/	
a	button /bʌtən/	
to	buy /baɪ/	
to	call /kɔːl/	
(adj)	calm /kɑːm/	
a	campaign /kæmpeɪn/	
to	cancel /kænsəl/	
a	cap /kæp/	
( )	capital /kæpɪtəl/	
to	care /keə/	
to	carry /kærɪ/	
to	carry out	
a	case /keɪs/	
( )	cash /kæʃ/	

Word		Meaning		Word		Meaning

a	catalogue /kætəlɒg/	to	cost /kɒst/
(adj)	cautious /kɔːʃəs/	to	count /kaʊnt/
to	celebrate /seləbreɪt/	a	course /kɔːs/
a	chain /tʃeɪn/	(adj)	creative /kriːeɪtɪv/
a	chairperson /tʃeəpɜːsən/	( )	credit /kredɪt/
to	change /tʃeɪndʒ/	a	criterion /kraɪtɪərɪən/
to	charge /tʃɑːdʒ/	a	currency /kʌrənsɪ/
(adj)	cheap /tʃiːp/	a	customer /kʌstəmə/
to	check /tʃek/		
to	choose /tʃuːz/	(adv)	daily /deɪlɪ/
to	claim /kleɪm/	(adj)	dangerous /deɪndʒərəs/
to	clean /kliːn/	a	deal /diːl/
a	client /klaɪənt/	to	deal with
to	close /kləʊz/	a	dealer
to	close down	a	debt /det/
a	colleague /kɒliːg/	to	decide /dɪsaɪd/
(adj)	comfortable /kʌmftəbəl/	a	decision /dɪsɪʒən/
to	comment /kɒment/	(adj)	decisive /dɪsaɪsɪv/
a	commission /kəmɪʃən/	to	define /dɪfaɪn/
( )	communication /kəmjuːnɪkeɪʃən/	to	delay /dɪleɪ/
a	company /kʌmpənɪ/	to	deliver /dɪlɪvə/
to	compare /kəmpeə/	a	delivery
( )	compensation /kɒmpənseɪʃən/	to	demand /dɪmɑːnd/
to	compete /kəmpiːt/	a	department /dɪpɑːtmənt/
(adj)	competitive /kəmpetɪtɪv/	to	depend on /dɪpend/
a	competitor /kəmpetɪtə/	to	design /dɪzaɪn/
a	complaint /kəmpleɪnt/	a	desk /desk/
to	complete /kəmpliːt/	a	detail /diːteɪl/
a	component /kəmpəʊnənt/	to	develop /dɪveləp/
a	conference /kɒnfərəns/	a	development
to	confirm /kənfɜːm/	(adj)	difficult /dɪfɪkəlt/
to	connect /kənekt/	to	disagree /dɪsəgriː/
to	consist of /kənsɪst/	a	discount /dɪskaʊnt/
a	consultant /kənsʌltənt/	to	discuss /dɪskʌs/
a	consumer /kənsjuːmə/	to	dismiss /dɪsmɪs/
to	contact /kɒntækt/	to	dispatch /dɪspætʃ/
to	contain /kənteɪn/	to	display /dɪspleɪ/
a	container	a	distance /dɪstəns/
to	continue /kəntɪnjuː/	to	distribute /dɪstrɪbjuːt/
a	contract /kɒntrækt/	(adj)	domestic /dəmestɪk/
to	control /kəntrəʊl/	to	drop /drɒp/
(adj)	convenient /kənviːnɪənt/	(prep)	due to /djuː/
a	conveyor belt /kənveɪə/		
a	copy /kɒpɪ/	to	earn /ɜːn/
a	corner /kɔːnə/	(adj)	easy /iːzɪ/
( )	correspondence /kɒrɪspɒndəns/	(adj)	economical /iːkənɒmɪkəl/
(n.pl.)	cosmetics /kɒzmetɪks/	( )	education /edjʊkeɪʃən/
		(adj)	efficient /ɪfɪʃənt/
		to	encourage /ɪnkʌrɪdʒ/
		an	end /end/
		an	end-user
		an	engineer /endʒɪnɪə/
		to	enjoy /ɪndʒɔɪ/

Word	Meaning		Word	Meaning

to	entertain /entəteɪn/		to	handle
an	entrance /entrəns/		(adj)	hard-working /hɒːd-wɜːkɪŋ/
an	environment /ɪnvaɪrənmənt/		(n.pl.)	headquarters /hedkwɔːtəz/
( )	equipment /əkwɪpmənt/		( )	health /helθ/
to	evaluate /ɪvæljuːeɪt/		a	hi-fi /haɪ-faɪ/
an	event /ɪvent/		(adj)	high /haɪ/
(prep)	except /eksept/		to	hit /hɪt/
(adj)	exclusive /ɪkskluːsɪv/		to	hold /həʊld/
to	excuse /ɪkskjuːz/		a	hole /həʊl/
an	exhibition /eksɪbɪʃən/		(adj)	honest /ɒnɪst/
(adj)	existing /ɪgsɪstɪŋ/		(adj)	huge /hjuːdʒ/
to	expand /ɪkspænd/			
an	expense /ɪkspens/		an	idea /aɪdɪə/
(adj)	expensive /ɪkspensɪv/		(adj)	ill /ɪl/
(adj)	experienced /ɪkspɪərɪənst/		an	image /ɪmɪdʒ/
to	explain /ɪkspleɪn/		to	import /ɪmpɔːt/
to	export /ɪkspɔːt/		(adj)	important /ɪmpɔːtənt/
			to	improve /ɪmpruːv/
a	facility /fəsɪlɪtɪ/			in charge of
a	factory /fæktərɪ/		to	include /ɪnkluːd/
to	fall /fɔːl/		to	increase /ɪnkriːs/
(adj)	famous /feɪməs/		an	individual /ɪndɪvɪdjʊəl/
a	fan /fæn/		an	industrialist /ɪndʌstrɪəlɪst/
(adj)	fast /fɑːst/		an	industry /ɪndəstrɪ/
a	feature /fiːtʃə/		( )	inflation /ɪnfleɪʃən/
a	figure /fɪgə/		to	inform /ɪnfɔːm/
to	fill in /fɪl/		( )	information /ɪnfəmeɪʃən/
to	fill out		to	inquire /ɪnkwaɪə/
(adv)	finally /faɪnəlɪ/		to	insert /ɪnsɜːt/
( )	finance /faɪnæns/		to	install /ɪnstɔːl/
to	find out /faɪnd/		( )	insurance /ɪnʃʊərəns/
to	finish /fɪnɪʃ/		( )	interest /ɪntərest/
to	fix /fɪks/		(adj)	interested in /ɪntərestɪd/
( )	flexibility /fleksɪbɪlɪtɪ/		(adj)	internal /ɪntɜːnəl/
a	flight /flaɪt/		to	invent /ɪnvent/
a	forecast /fɔːkɑːst/		to	invest /ɪnvest/
a	foreman /fɔːmən/		an	investment /ɪnvestmənt/
to	forget /fəget/		to	invite /ɪnvaɪt/
a	form /fɔːm/		an	invoice /ɪnvɔɪs/
to	found /faʊnd/		( )	iron /aɪən/
( )	freedom /friːdəm/			
(adj)	full /fʊl/		to	join /dʒɔɪn/
a	fund /fʌnd/			
			(adj)	keen on /kiːn/
(n.pl.)	goods /gʊdz/		to	keep /kiːp/
a	government /gʌvənmənt/		a	keyboard /kiːbɔːd/
(adj)	grateful /greɪtfʊl/		a	knob /nɒb/
a	group /gruːp/			
to	guarantee /gærəntiː/		( )	labour /leɪbə/
a	handle /hændəl/			

Word	Meaning		Word	Meaning
(adj)	last /lɑːst/		to	motivate /məʊtɪveɪt/
(adj)	latest /leɪtɪst/		to	move /muːv/
to	launch /lɔːntʃ/			
a	law /lɔː/		to	nationalize /næʃənəlaɪz/
to	lay off /leɪ/		(adj)	natural /nætʃərəl/
(adj)	leading /liːdɪŋ/		(prep)	near /nɪə/
a	leaflet /liːflɪt/		(adv)	nearly /nɪəlɪ/
( )	leather /leðə/		(adj)	necessary /nesəserɪ/
(adj)	left /left/		to	need /nɪːd/
(adj)	legal /liːgəl/		to	negotiate /nəgəʊʃɪeɪt/
to	lend /lend/		a	network /netwɜːk/
to	let someone know		a	newsletter /njuːzletə/
a	lever /liːvə/		(prep)	next to /nekst/
a	library /laɪbrərɪ/		a	note /nəʊt/
a	lid /lɪd/			
a	list /lɪst/		to	offer /ɒfə/
a	loan /ləʊn/		an	office /ɒfɪs/
(adj)	local /ləʊkəl/		(adj)	old /əʊld/
a	lock /lɒk/		to	open /əʊpən/
(adj)	long-lasting /lɒŋ-lɑːstɪŋ/		(adj)	open-minded /-maɪndɪd/
to	look after /lʊk/		to	operate /ɒpəreɪt/
to	look at		an	opinion /əpɪnjən/
to	look for		an	opportunity /ɒpətjuːnɪtɪ/
to	look forward to /fɔːwəd/		(prep)	opposite /ɒpəzɪt/
to	lose /luːz/		an	option /ɒpʃən/
a	loss /lɒs/		to	order /ɔːdə/
to	lower /ləʊwə/		(adj)	ordinary /ɔːdɪnrɪ/
( )	luxury /lʌkʃərɪ/		to	organize /ɔːgənaɪz/
			an	outline /aʊtlaɪn/
a	machine /məʃiːn/		( )	output /aʊtpʊt/
(adj)	main /meɪn/		(prep)	outside /aʊtsaɪd/
(adj)	major /meɪdʒə/		an	oven /ʌvən/
to	manage /mænɪdʒ/		an	overhead /əʊvəhed/
( )	management		( )	overtime /əʊvətaɪm/
	/mænɪdʒmənt/		to	owe /əʊ/
a	manager /mænɪdʒə/		to	own /əʊn/
( )	manpower /mænpaʊə/			
to	manufacture		to	pack /pæk/
	/mænjəfæktʃə/		( )	packaging /pækɪdʒɪŋ/
a	market /mɑːkɪt/		a	parent /peərənt/
(adj)	mass /mæs/		a	park /pɑːk/
a	material /mətɪərɪəl/		to	pass on /pɑːs/
a	maximum /mæksɪməm/		(adj)	patient /peɪʃənt/
to	mean /miːn/		to	pay back /peɪ/
(adj)	medium /miːdɪəm/		a	pension /penʃən/
to	meet /miːt/		a	performance
a	meeting /miːtɪŋ/			/pəfɔːməns/
a	memo /meməʊ/		( )	permission /pəmɪʃən/
to	mention /menʃən/		(adj)	personal /pɜːsənəl/
to	merge with /mɜːdʒ/		( )	personnel /pɜːsənel/
a	message /mesɪdʒ/		a	plan /plæn/
to	mind /maɪnd/		a	plant /plɑːnt/
(adj)	modern /mɒdən/		(adj)	popular /pɒpjələ/
to	modernize /mɒdənaɪz/		(adj)	portable /pɔːtəbəl/

Word	Meaning	Word	Meaning

a	position /pəzıʃən/	to	recruit /rıkruːt/
(adj)	possible /pɒsıbəl/	to	reduce /rıdjuːs/
to	post /pəʊst/	a	reduction /rıdʌkʃən/
a	post office /-ɒfıs/	to	refill /riːfıl/
to	pour /pɔː/	to	refund /riːfʌnd/
( )	power /paʊə/	to	refuse /rıfjuːz/
(adj)	powerful /paʊəfʊl/	(prep)	regarding /rıgɑːdıŋ/
to	prepare /prəpeə/	(n.pl.)	regards
to	present /prəzent/	(adj)	regular /regjələ/
a	presentation /prezənteıʃən/	(n.pl.)	relations /rıleıʃənz/
to	press /pres/	(adj)	reliable /rılaıəbəl/
( )	press	to	remain /rımeın/
a	price /praıs/	to	remove /rımuːv/
to	privatize /praıvətaız/	to	rent /rent/
a	problem /prɒbləm/	to	repay /rıpeı/
a	process /prəʊses/	to	replace /rıpleıs/
to	produce /prədjuːs/	to	reply /rıplaı/
a	product /prɒdʌkt/	to	report /rıpɔːt/
( )	productivity /prɒdʌktıvıtı/	a	representative /reprızentətıv/
a	profit /prɒfıt/	a	reputation /repjuːteıʃən/
a	programme /prəʊgræm/	to	request /rıkwest/
( )	progress /prəʊgres/	to	require /rıkwaıə/
to	promise /prɒmıs/	( )	research /rısɜːtʃ/
to	promote /prəməʊt/	a	reservation /rezəveıʃən/
a	promotion /prəməʊʃən/	to	reserve /rızɜːv/
a	property /prɒpətı/	a	resource /rızɔːs/
to	propose /prəpəʊz/	(adj)	responsible for /rıspɒnsıbəl/
to	provide /prəvaıd/	to	restrict /rıstrıkt/
( )	publicity /pʌblısıtı/	( )	retail /riːteıl/
to	purchase /pɜːtʃıs/	to	retire /rıtaıə/
a	purpose /pɜːpəs/	(adj)	right /raıt/
to	push /pʊʃ/	to	rise /raız/
to	put off /pʊt/	a	risk /rısk/
to	put s.o. through to /θruː/	( )	rubber /rʌbə/
		to	run /rʌn/
a	quality /kwɒlıtı/	to	run out of
a	quantity /kwɒntıtı/		
(adj)	quiet /kwaıət/	to	sack /sæk/
		(adj)	safe /seıf/
to	raise /reız/	( )	safety /seıftı/
a	range /reınʒ/	a	salary /sælərı/
(adv)	rapidly /ræpıdlı/	a	sale /seıl/
a	rate /reıt/	( )	satisfaction /sætısfækʃən/
to	realize /rıəlaız/	to	satisfy /sætısfaı/
a	reason /reːzən/	to	save /seıv/
a	receipt /rısiːt/	a	scheme /skiːm/
to	receive /rısiːv/	a	screen /skriːn/
(adj)	recent /riːsənt/	a	season /siːzən/
a	receptionist /rısepʃənıst/	(adj)	second-hand /sekənd-hænd/
to	recognize /rekəgnaız/	to	select /sılekt/
to	recommend /rekəmend/		

Word		Meaning	Word		Meaning
to	sell /sel/		a	tax /tæks/	
to	send /send/		( )	technology /teknɒlədʒɪ/	
(adj)	serious /sɪərɪəs/		to	test /test/	
to	serve /sɜːv/		(adj)	thick /θɪk/	
to	service /sɜːvɪs/		(adj)	thin /θɪn/	
a	service		to	think /θɪŋk/	
to	set up /set/		(adj)	thirsty /θɜːstɪ/	
a	shape /ʃeɪp/		(adj)	thorough /θʌrə/	
to	share /ʃeə/		to	throw away /θrəʊ/	
a	share		to	tighten /taɪtən/	
a	shareholder /ʃeəhəʊldə/		(adj)	tiny /taɪnɪ/	
(adv)	sharply /ʃɒːplɪ/		a	total /təʊtəl/	
to	show /ʃəʊ/		(adj)	tough /tʌf/	
a	side /saɪd/		a	tour /tʊə/, /tɔː(r)/	
to	sign /saɪn/		a	trade fair /treɪd feə/	
a	situation /sɪtjuːeɪʃən/		to	train /treɪn/	
a	size /saɪz/		to	transfer /trænsfɜː/	
(adj)	skilled /skɪld/		to	transmit /trænzmɪt/	
(adv)	slightly /slaɪtlɪ/		( )	transport /trænspɔːt/	
(adv)	slowly /sləʊlɪ/		to	travel /trævəl/	
(adj)	sociable /səʊʃəbəl/		a	travel agent	
a	solution /səluːʃən/		a	trip /trɪp/	
to	solve /sɒlv/		a	tube /tjuːb/	
(adv)	soon /suːn/		a	turnover /tɜːnəʊvə/	
(adj)	sorry /sɒrɪ/		a	type /taɪp/	
to	specialize /speʃəlaɪz/				
(adj)	specific /spəsɪfɪk/		(adj)	understanding /ʌndəstændɪŋ/	
to	spell /spel/		( )	unemployment /ʌnemplɔɪmənt/	
to	spend /spend/				
( )	staff /stɑːf/		(adj)	unique /juːniːk/	
a	stand /stænd/		(adj)	unusual /ʌnjuːʒʊəl/	
to	stand at		(adj)	up-market /ʌpmɑːkɪt/	
a	state /steɪt/		(adj)	useful /juːsfʊl/	
to	stay /steɪ/				
( )	steel /stiːl/		(adj)	valuable /væljəbəl/	
( )	stock /stɒk/		a	value /væljuː/	
a	stock market		a	visit /vɪzɪt/	
( )	stress /stres/		a	visitor /vɪzɪtə(r)/	
a	strike /straɪk/				
( )	string /strɪŋ/		a	wage /weɪdʒ/	
a	subsidiary /səbsɪdʒərɪ/		a	warehouse /weəhaʊs/	
to	suggest /sədʒest/		to	wash /wɒʃ/	
to	suit /suːt/		to	waste /weɪst	
to	supervise /suːpəvaɪz/		to	wear /weə/	
a	supplier /səplaɪə/		(adj)	well-known /wel-nəʊn/	
to	supply		(adj)	whole /həʊl/	
to	support /səpɔːt/		a	wholesaler /həʊlseɪlə/	
(adj)	sure /ʃɔː(r)/		to	win /wɪn/	
a	survey /sɜːveɪ/		to	withdraw /wɪðdrɔː/	
a	switch /swɪtʃ/		to	worry /wʌrɪ/	
			(adj)	worth /wɜːθ/	
a	takeover /teɪkəʊvə/		(adj)	wrong /rɒŋ/	
a	target /tɑːgɪt/				